DONALD J TRUMP:

The Innovative Genius Carving an Indelible Legacy.

Jumel Pluviose

DONALD J TRUMP: The Innovative Genius Carving an Indelible Legacy.

TABLE OF CONTENTS

Acknowledgements

I stand at the fruition of a lifelong dream, and as I embark on this journey as an author, there are countless individuals whose steady support and belief in me have made this moment possible.

Dedication

To my cherished family and beloved friends, your encouragement, laughter, and shared moments have been the true inspiration behind this book. With gratitude for the warmth of your presence, idedicate these words to you, knowing that our stories will continue to interwine on every page of life.

Foreword

Donald Trump's presidency no doubt left a mark on the US, and indeed global democracy and politics. There were several points during Trump's presidency that many of us had to rethink governance and the legal system. Donald Trump went into an open battle with the United States government and it is still ongoing. As he campaigns for re-election in 2024. This book serves as an excellent material to reflect on Donald Trump, the man, the president and his presidency, before, during and after his time serving in the white house.

Understanding the impact Trump has had on the US politics and global politics takes understanding the man himself, the government of the nation within which he operates, and the circumstances surrounding him at different stages of his life. The position of President of the United State holds so much significance that anyone who has attained such height must be of some substance and some level of integrity and good standing. Amidst the impeachments and several legal battles, whether or not Trump represents the ideals of a United States president is one of two things; a worthy man widely misunderstood or an incredibly well played out scheme to hijack power.

The book objectively presents the facts taking a neutral stance while proposing some interpretations of the Trump phenomena. Beyond the headlines and popular opinions, the book takes a bold step of looking at the other side of the story and tries to draw deeper insight. It draws from diverse resources in order to present an understanding of a complex character and a rather turbulent era.

Preface

In a world of constant record breaking, relentless opinions, and heated debates, it is a rare endeavor to embark upon a journey of objective inquiry. This book seeks to traverse that path, guided by a commitment to impartiality and neutrality. Its aim is not to take sides, to praise or condemn, but rather to illuminate the complex tapestry of one individual's impact on a nation and the world.

Donald J. Trump, a name that invokes a myriad of emotions, stands as a figure emblematic of controversy and transformation. The pages that follow do not harbor intentions of molding him into a hero or a villain. Rather, they intend to serve as a mirror reflecting the intricate facets of a man who has indelibly marked the annals of American history. It is a narrative not woven from personal opinions or judgments, but from the threads of observation, analysis, and respectful contemplation.

In a society deeply divided along ideological lines, the pursuit of understanding can be overshadowed by the clamor of partisanship. This book, in its exploration, aspires to rise above the cacophony, providing a space for introspection and examination. It neither endeavors to undermine the accomplishments of the past, nor to predict the course of the future. Instead, it seeks to cast a discerning light on the intricate dance between an individual and a nation, between a personality and a presidency.

Section I
The Innovative Genius

Understanding Trump's Personality Traits.

For the purpose of this book, I will first explore the concept of genius, some characteristics of it, and different factors that contribute to the development of a genius. It will also focus on how environment, upbringing, and opportunities play a major role in creating a genius. This will help assess if Trump meets the criteria to be described as a genius.

Chapter I
What is a genius?

A genius is an individual possessing both exceptional intelligence and remarkable creativity, qualities that are not commonly found in many intelligent people. Although some individuals are creative, they may lack the intellectual capacity necessary to fully utilize their creativity (Simonton, 2021). Furthermore, being a genius involves having a unique approach to problem-solving and being able to generate groundbreaking ideas that challenge the conventional ways of thinking. Most of the geniuses have things they have created, and they are different from what people see or view. Additionally, most geniuses have made inventions that have helped to improve the lives of people.

While some people use a person's IQ as a gauge for determining if they are a genius, this method is considered imperfect by many. Rather, many individuals believe that the most accurate measure of a genius lies in the outcomes they produce in their lifetime, despite the limitations of IQ tests. Most of these individuals have talents in multiple fields and can sometimes be considered polymaths (Simonton, 2021). However, a genius is defined as someone with original and exceptional insight into the work that someone does or even an endeavor that goes beyond human understanding and expectations. A genius sets new standards for the future and comes up with better methods of operation, and he also has outstanding abilities compared to the ability of the people they are competing with. Most of the time, a genius is believed to be someone with a remarkable intellectual or even creative function or other natural ability.

Characteristics of a Genius

A genius has a curious mind. One needs to possess a high degree of curiosity to achieve excellence. Through having a highly inquisitive nature, a person is more likely to develop new ways of thinking to uncover previously unexplored ideas. Many geniuses are deemed often to pursue knowledge in some obsessive way, which is beyond what an average person can consider reasonable (Akhmatkhonovna, 2021). Also, geniuses are abstract thinkers. Many people who have geniuses' traits are said to think about problems and concepts in a much more dynamic way. As a result, only some geniuses are likely to accept information and facts on face value. Instead, such people will want to defy and test conservative thinking. Talking to someone with genius traits can be challenging as they may wish to keep challenging their thinking. Many of the people who are geniuses keep on challenging other people's ideas because they believe in themselves so much and trust that they are always right.

In addition, geniuses have the traits of risk-takers. People that are so much innovative will want to push boundaries. Such people are not satisfied with taking a safe route, especially when they feel close to making a certain discovery. This form of approach to life at many times could mean that they put themselves at risk, whether physically or regarding the progression of their carrier, and this, in the end, can lead to ground-breaking work (Vecco, 2020). Most geniuses are thinkers to the core in all aspects. Most minds of people who are geniuses are always on the move, and thoughts are always constantly flowing through them. It is not that thoughts run through their mind constantly, but they think about a problem in a deeper way and from different perspectives.

With all the perspectives, they can understand a problem much better and find not just a solution to something, but they can innovate through it. Most geniuses when faced with a certain problem they work hard to make sure that they solve the problem and bring up a long-lasting solution.

Moreover, geniuses have an insatiable appetite for knowledge. People with genius minds hunger for knowledge, and they will go out of the expected way to experiment and explore the possibilities in all the things that run into their minds. Many genius people can learn something new every day, or they are deeply introspecting about something they have been thinking about (Coles, 2020). Also, most geniuses do admit that they don't know whatever they don't know. It is said that the less intelligent a person is, the more people overestimate their mental abilities. Most geniuses hope to learn more about the things they don't know much about and always hope to learn.

In most cases, genius people tend to be more individualistic than others. Many geniuses love spending time with themselves and introspecting about their things and thoughts. Many do not connect with people on several things they lack interest in because they mostly speak whenever they feel they need to. Most of the genius people feel that they should just be settled alone and many times they are just locked in their rooms (Coles, 2020). There are other people with a genius mind and all they think of is themselves and people who are so close to them. Most of the genius people will be awake until late at night and they hate waking up in the morning hours.

Chapter II

Exploring some prominent Geniuses realms and achievements in the World.

The concept of genius is highly subjective and difficult to quantify. It is also important to note that intelligence and success come in different forms. The era, context, and field in which intelligence and success are identified, considered, or recognized must be taken into consideration. Some highly intelligent people have made groundbreaking discoveries that impact the whole world while others make discoveries or move the notch just one bar higher still impact a group of people's lives. Will it be appropriate to compare individuals' achievements solely based on a narrow set of criteria? I have no intention to credit one with no merit or diminish the solid legacy of the prominent geniuses. It is only a quest to discover.

One of the most prominent geniuses in the world is Isaac Newton. Newton was an exceptional polymath who excelled in physics, mathematics, astronomy, and alchemy due to his outstanding genius. He has been one of the most influential and one of greatest scientists to have ever lived. His scientific work gave birth to a lot of today's modern technology (Smith, 2008).

Galileo Galilei, a renowned astronomer and physicist, was also a distinguished mathematician who can be considered as a genius. He is widely regarded as the "father of modern astronomy" due to his significant contributions to the scientific revolution. Also, he is remembered for his work inventing a telescope and the military compass (Machamer and Miller, 2021).

Thomas Alva Edison was also a great investor and businessman who helped build the American economy. He is said to be the mastermind behind the many discoveries and the front-runner of the American technological revolution. It is through him that a lot of scientific discoveries have been found in the US. Through him the industries as well as the economy thrived fast because of the changes that he brought. Leonardo da Vinci, an architect, mathematician, musician, and writer was another renowned genius. Through him modern America was built as well as modern architectural designs. He is said to have been the first to dissect a human body.

Stephen Hawking is a theoretical physicist, cosmologist and director of research at Centre for theoretical Cosmology, University of Cambridge in the United Kingdom. He developed several theories which served as foundation for groundbreaking discoveries and understanding about the universe (Hawking, 2009). He also contributed significantly to increasing the popularity of science, through his book publications, lectures and even appearances in a popular TV show, "The Big Bang Theory". He has an exceptional ability to effectively communicate science in an appealing manner to the lay person.

Most of our contemporary personalities have been working tirelessly and making unimaginable and practical discoveries/revolutions/groundbreakings that are impacting the daily living in the universe. Should they be recognized as geniuses now or should they wait for their legacies to evolve after a number of years or after death?

What one can say about:

Elon Musk: an entrepreneur, engineer, and inventor. Elon Musk is the founder of spaceX, Telsa, Neuralink, and the boring company. Elon Musk is "it" when it comes to electric cars (which I don't have one yet), space exploration (who knows I might take a tour there), and renewable energy.

Malala Yousafzai: She is known for advocacy for girls' education and women's rights. Malala Yousafzai is an activist and Nobel laureate. She has become a global symbol of empowerment since she survived an assassination attempt by the Taliban 2012.

Greta Thunberg: A climate activist, gained international attention for her protests and activism demanding action on climate change. She has been nominated for the Nobel peace prize and has inspired a global movement of young people fighting for a sustainable future.

Yoshua Bengio: A computer scientist and AI (Artificial Intelligence) researcher, he is one of the pioneers of deep learning, a subfield of machine learning. He is a professor of computer science at University of Montreal. His research has contributed significantly to artificial intelligence and natural language processing. He was awarded the Turing Award, considered the Nobel prize of computer science, in 2018.

Another prominent genius whose superior intelligence and ability had made groundbreaking in the area of human rights ensuring justice for all, is **General Jean Jacques Dessalines**. Jean Jacques Dessalines was born in slavery in the island of Hispaniola, now known as Haiti. Slavery was dehumanizing human beings by subduing them to profound suffering and exploitation. Their basic right was denied, and they were treated as properties. Jean Jacques Dessalines grew up believing in the fundamental rights of all individuals, regardless of their race, gender, or background. Jean Jacques Dessalines was a well-crafted Haitian revolutionary leader who fought tirelessly to end slavery and establish equality for all people not only in Haiti but in the world. Jean Jacques Dessalines played a significant role in the Haitian Revolution, which culminated in the establishment of Haiti as the first Black-led republic in the world. Dessalines' work in the area of human rights was groundbreaking and served as an inspiration to other revolutionary leaders throughout the world. His legacy continues to be felt today by all wherever human rights are transgressed. Jean Jacques Dessalines became the paragon of moral fortitude, embodying the essence of what it means to be a beacon of hope and a harbinger of change. His achievement resonates not only as milestones in the advancement of human rights and justice, but also a symphony of inspiration, compelling others to transcend their limits and to take up the mantle of leadership. His drive to achieve what seemed impossible to human imagination has galvanized a movement that transcends borders, cultures, and generations. A movement that dares to envision a world where fairness is not just an aspiration but an inalienable birthright.

Analyzing similarity of geniuses' personality traits.

In the quest of defining, classifying, or identifying what it means to be a genius, what genius do, or who can be considered as a genius, Artificial Intelligence (AI) has brought to light some explanations that I found to be very sound minded. Thanks to my son and my nephew who warned me to be friend with Artificial Intelligence for AI is readily capable to assist and available to open doors anytime and for anyone.

I asked AI to generate 5 main types of genius. The answer is as follow:

1. Creative Genius: This type of genius is characterized by an exceptional ability to innovate, create, and imagine novel ideas, art, and designs. Examples include Pablo Picasso, Leonardo da Vinci, and Albert Einstein.

2. Intellectual Genius: This type of genius is characterized by exceptional intellectual capabilities, high IQ, and academic achievement. Examples include Stephen Hawking, Marie Curie, and Isaac Newton.

3. Emotional Genius: Emotional geniuses possess an exceptional ability to understand, manage, and express their own emotions and the emotions of others. Examples include Oprah Winfrey, Dalai Lama, and Mother Teresa.

4. Athletic Genius: This type of genius is characterized by exceptional physical abilities and performance in sports. Examples include Michael Phelps, Serena Williams, and Usain Bolt.

5. Business Genius: Business geniuses possess exceptional entrepreneurial skills, strategic thinking, and vision. Examples include Steve Jobs, Warren Buffet, and Jeff Bezos.

In regards of the above-mentioned prominent and contemporary geniuses, all of them demonstrated exceptional abilities in their respective fields of evolvement. However, their areas of expertise and contributions to society are vastly different. Most of them are recognized for their groundbreaking discoveries in their fields, technical and scientific revolution, modern technology, modern architectural designs, environmental safeguard, and human rights. Some of their works impact the whole world population and some others might impact a more contained group of the world population.

Whether the genius work is local or global, scientific or creative, and ancient, modern, or contemporary, geniuses work for a variety of people or causes; it all depends on their interests and passions. Some geniuses work for themselves, conducting their own research or projects, and others may work for companies, institutions, or specific causes that align with their values, interests, and goals. Whatever the result of the use or application of the genius work, it doesn't de-classify the genius person as a genius. So often, the scientists have naïve curiosity to discover solution to problems, but other people use them to destroy. An example is biotechnology which was created to manipulate deadly pathogens or biological agents but has potential to be used as a bioweapon.

Indeed, a genius is a genius. Based on the characteristics of a genius, it's undisputable that all geniuses exhibit similar behaviors and or share most of the following traits: creativity, curiosity, intense focus, and persistency. See how my assistant AI explains those traits.

1. High levels of creativity: Geniuses are known for their exceptional ability to come up with new and innovative ideas. They are often highly creative individuals who can think outside the box and find unique solutions to problems.

2. Intense focus and determination: Geniuses tend to have a laser-like focus when it comes to pursuing their goals. They are highly motivated individuals who are not easily deterred by obstacles or setbacks.

3. Exceptional intelligence: Geniuses are often highly intelligent individuals who have a deep understanding of complex subjects. They have the ability to grasp abstract concepts quickly and easily and can often see connections and patterns that others miss.

4. Persistence and resilience: Geniuses are not deterred by failure. Instead, they see it as an opportunity to learn and grow. They are highly resilient individuals who are able to bounce back from setbacks and continue to pursue their goals.

5. Curiosity and a thirst for knowledge: Geniuses are often highly curious individuals who have a deep love of learning. They are constantly seeking new knowledge and experiences are always looking for ways to expand their understanding of the world around them.

Chapter III
Exploring the complex and perplex characteristics and traits of Mr. Donald J Trump.

Studying some remarkable traits of Donald J. Trump will enlighten the issue whether he is a real genius or is just a flamboyant self-proclaiming 'fine genius."

Unfolding Donald Trump early childhood wonders.

Donald J Trump was born on June 14, 1946, Donald John Trump was born in Queens, New York. His father, Fred Trump, was a very famous real estate entrepreneur. Fred Trump had German ancestry, while his wife and Donald Trump's mother, Mary McLeod, had Scottish origin. Donald was the fourth out of five siblings. At age 13 Donald Trump was sent to a military academy after misbehaving in school.

The historical records reveal a fascinating aspect of Donald Trump's early life: at the age of 13, he was sent to a military academy due to what was deemed as "misbehavior." This intriguing revelation beckons us to delve deeper into the actions that prompted such a consequential decision. What exactly constituted Donald Trump's misbehavior? The term itself, "misbehavior," carries an air of mystery, as it encompasses a wide array of possibilities, ranging from disruptive conduct to more complex and challenging behaviors.

Disruptive behaviors typically disrupt the harmonious flow of a household, classroom, or any social setting. They can manifest in various ways, such as incessant screaming, physical aggression, bullying of peers, defiance, or a consistent refusal to adhere to rules and directions. These behaviors can cause turmoil and disturbance, making it difficult for those around the individual to maintain a semblance of order and routine. One can't help but wonder if Donald Trump's misbehavior at that tender age involved such disruptive actions, potentially causing disruptions within his family or educational environment.

However, misbehavior can also encompass challenging behavior, which presents a different set of complexities. Challenging behavior arises when a child demonstrates a lack of interest in routine activities, struggles to find motivation to progress, or experiences difficulties focusing on instructions. In some cases, the child may exhibit advanced cognitive abilities or problem-solving skills that surpass the capabilities of their parents, family, or educational institution to effectively address their unique needs and demands. Could it be that Donald Trump's misbehavior fell within this realm of challenges? Perhaps his behavior reflected his exceptional cognitive abilities, his relentless curiosity about the world around him, or an unquenchable thirst for knowledge and growth.

Considering the multifaceted nature of misbehavior, it becomes increasingly captivating to speculate about the exact nature of Donald Trump's actions during his formative years. As an individual fortunate enough to witness the unfolding of Donald Trump's public life, encompassing his eventful tenure as the President of the United States, I find myself intrigued by the correlation between his past and present. It is as if the saying "We will be in life what we were on the school benches." resonates with his trajectory, suggesting that his misbehavior in his youth may have shaped the person he ultimately became.

Therefore, it is reasonable to assert that Donald Trump's misbehavior was likely a nuanced blend of disruptive and challenging behaviors, representative of the complexity and diversity of his character. This realization allows one to appreciate the intricate layers of his experiences, motivations, and aspirations, ultimately contributing to a more comprehensive understanding of his journey from a young cadet with misbehavior to a prominent figure on the global stage.

Who is Donald J Trump?

Donald Trump is primarily a businessman, television personality, and former President of the United States of America. Donald Trump is widely known for his career in real estate, having developed many high-profile properties around the world. He is also recognized for his role in the television show" The apprentice," where he served as the host and the executive producer. Donald Trump officially entered politics in 2015 when he announced his candidacy for President of the United States, running on a platform of populist nationalism. He was elected as the 45th President in 2016, and his tenure in office was marked by controversy and division. He left office in January 2021, and his legacy continues to be a subject of debate. Donald also the one President who didn't shake hand of the succeeding President of the United States.

Donald Trump's propelling core training

Donald Trump received his education at the New York Military Academy and the University of Pennsylvania's Wharton School of Finance and Commerce. Trump then joined the real estate and construction business even before graduating from college. Despite his family's affluence, Trump had to work in the lowest-level positions within his father's firm. As a young man, he took over his family business and changed its name to "The Trump Organization". After attending the Wharton School at the University of Pennsylvania, Maryanne Trump Barry, who is Donald's eldest sister, went on to serve as a United States district court judge from 1983 to 1999 and then until her retirement in 2011, she served as a judge on the United States Court of Appeals for the Third Circuit. After deciding to become a pilot, Trump's older brother, Fred, became the favorite to succeed his father. According to Donald Trump, Fred Trump died at the age of 43 due to alcoholism after an incident that caused him to abstain from drinking and smoking for the rest of his life (Donald Trump's life story: From hotel developer to president, 2021). In his book (Donald Trump, 1987),

Trump discusses his undergraduate career by saying that he also considered going to film school after he graduated from the New York Military Academy but ended up choosing the family real estate business.

In the late 1920s, Fred Trump began his construction business by building single-family in the Queens and Brooklyn boroughs of New York City. From the late 1940s to the late 1950s, he built thousands of residential units, primarily located in Brooklyn, with the help of a federal loan guaranteed to encourage the construction of affordable housing throughout. He also worked for the forces by building federally subsidized housing in Virginia and Pennsylvania for military personnel and shipyard workers during WWII. In 1954, the Senate Banking Committee investigated Fred for exploiting the loan-guarantee scheme by overestimating the price of his construction projects to secure larger loans from financial institutions and retain the disparity between the amount of credit and his actual construction costs. Fred acknowledged to a Senate committee in 1954 that the Beach Haven apartment complex in Brooklyn was built for $3.7 million less than the amount of his government-insured loan. Although he was never charged with a criminal offence, he could not receive government loan guarantees after that. As per a New York state investigation a decade later, Fred used the profit from a state-insured loan agreement to build a shopping mall that was his property. He could not obtain state financial assistance for residential constructions in Brooklyn's Coney Island neighborhood after repaying $1.2 million to the state.

Trump's education at the New York Military Academy provided him with discipline, structure, and leadership skills. This military-style training likely contributed to his assertive and commanding demeanor. Additionally, attending the Wharton School of Finance and Commerce at the University of Pennsylvania equipped him with a strong business background and knowledge of finance, which proved invaluable in his later ventures.

Donald Trump's upbringing and early experiences played a significant role in shaping him into the individual he is today. Growing up in a wealthy family, Trump was exposed to the world of real estate and construction from a young age. However, his father made him start from the lowest-level positions within the family business, teaching him the value of hard work and instilling a strong work ethic.

Taking over the family business at a relatively young age, Trump had to demonstrate his abilities and prove himself as a capable leader. This experience taught him resilience, decision- making skills, and the importance of strategic thinking. It also allowed him to build a reputation in the real estate and construction industry.

Trump's family background and connections also played a significant role in his development. His sister's successful career in the judiciary system and his brother's own tragic struggle with alcoholism likely influenced his drive to succeed and establish his own legacy. These experiences may have instilled in him a desire to excel and stand out in his own field.

Furthermore, Trump's encounters with challenges and controversies, such as the Senate Banking Committee investigating into his father's business practices, exposed him to the complexities of navigating legal and financial matters. These experiences likely honed his negotiation skills, resilience in the face of adversity, and ability to handle public scrutiny.

Overall, Donald Trump's upbringing, education, and early experiences in the real estate and construction industry provided him with a unique foundation that shaped him into the confident, ambitious, and determined individual he became.

Donald Trump's disruptive personality traits manifestation in business, television, and presidency

Donald Trump is a prominent business magnate; his approach to business was often confrontational and he has a reputation of being difficult. His disruptive character in business can be traced back to his early days as a real estate developer. He was known for his brash personality and aggressive business tactics, which often involved resentments, aggressive negotiation, litigations, and several lawsuits against him.

Donald Trump was the host of the reality TV show "The Apprentice," which aired from 2004 to 2015. Throughout his television career, his disruptive and aggressive personality was evident. On the show, Trump was known for his combative personality and aggressive management style. The essence of the show was clashing with contestants and Donald Trump was famous with his catchphrase, "You're fired!' He was also well known for his contentious relationships with the journalists and often accused the media of being biased against him. His disruptive and abrupt behavior was evident in the use of twitter to communicate directly with his followers, he usually used the platform to attack his critics.

Taking a quick look at staff clashing and turnover of Donald Trump's first few months of his presidency, one might wonder whether Donald Trump's 'misbehavior' meant that he can only function in chaos and if the environment is not, he would have at least to turn it into a drama /jungle queen house. Here are few high-profile members clashing with Trump and staff turnovers of his own administration and political party:

Trump accused his Attorney General, Jeff Sessions, one of his most loyal supporters, of disloyalty and ultimately forced him to resign because Sessions recused himself from the investigation into Russian interference in the 2016 election (Baker, Benner & Shear, 2018).

Trump clashed with his first Secretary of State, Rex Tillerson on several issues, including the Iran nuclear deal and the handling of the North Korean nuclear threat. Trump criticized Tillerson's negotiation skills and ultimately fired him via twitter (Mohammed and Heavey, 2018).

John Bolton was Trump's National Security Advisor. He clashed with Trump on several key issue, including North Korea and Iran.

Despite his reputation of hawkish foreign policy expert, he was fired by Trump for disagreement over policy (Alfaro, 2022).

The Speaker of the House, Paul Rayan, was a key ally of Trump in Congress. Ryan clashed with Trump over issues such as the repeal of the Affordable Care Act and the president's inflammatory rhetoric. The clash caused Ryan not to seek re-election in 2018. Ryan continues to openly criticize trump (Marchese, 2023).

Mitt Romney, a former Republican presidential candidate and now a sitting senator from Utah, has been one of Trump's most vocal Republican critics (Kapur, 2023).

Some of the most notable departures from the Trump administration include:

Michael Flynn, Trump's first National Security Advisor, resigned after just 24 days on the job due to his contacts with Russian officials.

Sean Spicer, Trump's first Press Secretary, resigned after just six months, citing his disagreements with Trump's decision to appoint Anthony Scaramucci as Communication Director.

Reince Priebus, Trump's first Chief of Staff, resigned after just six months, citing his disagreements with Trump's leadership style.

Gary Cohn, Trump's top economic advisor, resigned after disagreeing with Trump's decision to impose tariffs on steel and aluminum imports.

John Kelly, Trump's second Chief of Staff, resigned after just 17 months, citing his frustration with Trump's management style. He also continued to speak out against Trump after his resignation (Helmore, 2020).

These high-profile departures, along with numerous other lower-level resignations, contributed to a sense of chaos and instability within the Trump's administration.

Donald Trump's disruptive behavior is only getting stronger and more effective, but not going away; it advanced from the school bench to business dealing, TV show production, then presidency administration. His presidency was known for his unconventional approach to politics, which often involved controversial statements and policies. Trump's disruptive character flowed throughout his presidency, which was marked by several high-profile case controversies, including his handling of the COVID-19 pandemic, his immigration policies, and his relationship with the media.

In conclusion, Donald Trump's assertive and unconventional approach, evident in his business dealings, television career, and presidency, has left a lasting impact on the political landscape. While his disruptive personality traits have garnered criticism, they have also brought attention to important issues and sparkled conversations that may have otherwise been overlooked. Trump's ability to challenge the status quo and address contentious topics has resonated with a significant portion of the population, leading to a dedicated base of supporters. Despite the controversies surrounding his tenure, it is undeniable that Trump's disruptive character has stimulated political engagement and discourse, encouraging a reevaluation of established norms. Whether viewed positively or negatively, his influence has undoubtedly left a significant imprint on the realms of business, entertainment, and politics.

Could it be argued that Donald Trump faced difficulties in maintaining focus or staying on task due to a lack of motivation or interest? Absolutely not! Given the remarkable accomplishments he has achieved throughout his life, I am firmly convinced that Mr. Trump's 'misbehavior' cannot be attributed to any such challenges in focusing on his endeavors.

Nevertheless, it is important to acknowledge that I do not possess the professional expertise to diagnose any potential conditions, nor do I possess extrasensory abilities to uncover matters beyond our physical senses. Even if a qualified psychiatrist, whether officially recognized or working in secrecy, were to have labeled him with conditions such as bipolar disorder or obsessive-compulsive disorder, such information would remain confidential and inaccessible. Instead, I would anticipate the focus shifting towards the release of his tax records following the conclusion of his presidency and the electoral process. It is my personal belief that a significant portion of the human population, whether diagnosed or not, grapples with various degrees of mental health challenges. Consequently, it is conceivable that Donald Trump, like any other human being, may also be subject to certain mental ailments. If his "misbehavior" were indeed linked to a mental health issue, I would assume that it was well-managed.

From one perspective, the designation of "misbehavior" attributed to Donald Trump continues to perplex and cause unease among those who seek detailed information. Conversely, for those who are patient, attentive, and willing to observe the complete unfolding of events, such a characterization remains undisturbed and composed.

When considering this unfolding narrative of "misbehavior," I firmly believe that Donald Trump's behavior was inherently challenging in the sense that he operated at a faster and more advanced pace than those surrounding him. A thorough examination of his business dealings, production of television shows, and presidential administration will continue to shed light on this perspective.

Donald Trump's philosophical strategies and characteristic traits might have interpreted as 'misbehavior'.

Donald Trump's life as a businessman, celebrity persona, and the 45th President of the United States was marked by a unique set of philosophical strategies and characteristic traits that garnered both admiration and criticism. From his unorthodox communication style to his policy decisions, Trump's approach often sparked controversy and invited interpretations of misbehavior. Delving into Trump's philosophical strategies, characteristic traits, and leadership style will reveal a deeper understanding of how his actions were perceived as "misbehavior."

Superiority Complex- Believing that he is superior to all other human and acting as such.

One of defining characteristics of Trump's persona is his tendency to present himself as superior to others and act as such. Trump has long been known for his brash personality. He presents himself as a bold, decisive leader who is not afraid to take risks and make tough decisions. He has also been known to tout his wealth and success as evidence of his superiority, and to belittle those who he perceives as being inferior. His famous phrase "You're fired" on his TV show conveys a sense of power, authority, and superiority over others. Trump surrounds himself with individuals who are loyal to him, rather than those who are the most qualified or competent for the job. He is known to make decisions based on his gut instinct and personal preference, rather than objective evidence or expert advice. Donald Trump believes and acts as if he is above the law by ignoring norms and rules that apply to other politicians and public figures. It's a standard practice for the presidential candidates to release their taxes. In the case of Donald Trump "No tax" (Debusmann Jr and Levinson-King, 2022).

Could following examples be considered as contributing factors that might swell his ego to feel and believe that he is superior to others?

Assertive and bold personality: Donald Trump's assertive and bold personality was evident throughout his life. One notable example of his assertiveness was his approach to international trade. He took strong stand on renegotiating trade deals, such as the North American Free Trade Agreement (NAFTA), which he believed were unfavorable to American interest. He boldly pushed for the replacement of NAFTA with the United States-Mexico-Canada Agreement (USMCA), asserting that it would protect American jobs and promote fairer trade practices. Trump's fearless determination and willingness to challenge established norms showcased his assertive and bold nature, leaving a lasting impact on both domestic and international affairs (Office of the United States Trade Representatie).

Public speaking skills: Donald Trump's public speaking skills are truly remarkable. With his powerful and compelling rhetoric, he can captivate any audience. Trump's confident and bold speaking personality exudes a persuasive aura that signals his sense of superiority. His speeches are often filled with strong and assertive statements, leaving a lasting impact on his listeners. Whether addressing his supporters or delivering a keynote address, Trump's ability to commend attention and deliver his message with conviction is undeniable. His public speaking prowess has played a significant role in shaping his political career and connecting with his base.

Resilience: Donald Trump's resilience is a defining characteristic trait that has been tested throughout his professional life. From weathering multiple bankruptcies (American Bankruptcy Institute) to weathering numerous scandals, he has consistently demonstrated his ability to bounce back and forge ahead. Despite setbacks that would have derailed many others, Trump has shown an unwavering confidence, has propelled him forward and enabled him to navigate through challenging situations. It is this remarkable ability to persevere in the face of adversity that some interpret as a testament to his superior resilience, shaping his reputation as a formidable force in the world of business and politics.

Business acumen: Donald Trump's business acumen is undeniable impressive, as evidenced by the vast empire he has built over the years. From real estate developments to casinos, golf courses, beauty pageants, and various other ventures, his entrepreneurial prowess is hard to overlook. Many admire his ability to navigate the complex world of business and turn opportunities into lucrative endeavors. However, it is important to note that while Trump's business success has garnered admiration from some, it has also faced challenges and criticism. The belief in his superiority, often observed in his actions and demeanor, can be attributed to the tangible examples of self-achievement he has accumulated throughout his career. These accomplishments have undoubtedly shaped his perspective and reinforced his confidence, even in the face of scrutiny. Whether one agrees or disagrees with his self-perceived superiority, there is no denying the impact his business acumen has had on his life and the way he approaches both business and politics.

Setting high standards and boasting about himself: Setting high standards and showcasing his achievements are notable aspects of Donald Trump's persona throughout his career as a businessman, reality TV star, and politician. Trump once expressed, "I have a penchant for thinking big. If you're going to think at all, you might as well think big." He consistently emphasized the pursuit of excellence, admitting, "I aim for perfection, and when I fall short, I feel deeply disappointed." Donald Trump frequently touted the exceptional quality of his properties, asserting that his buildings and resorts were unrivaled worldwide. His reputation for self-promotion and boasting about his accomplishments precedes him. For instance, he declared himself the "best dealmaker" globally (Rushe, 2020) and claimed to possess a "remarkably high IQ." Through shows like "The Apprentice," Trump challenged conventional business education by introducing a competitive format in which participants engaged in various business tasks to vie for a job within his organization. The program portrayed Trump as a shrewd entrepreneur and charismatic leader, solidifying his image as a successful businessperson. While his tendency to boast has attracted criticism, with accusations of narcissism and excessive self-promotion, it is undeniable that Donald Trump establishes lofty standards, strives for and attains excellence, and constructs opulent establishments.

Challenging the status quo: Challenging the established norms and traditions, Donald Trump has consistently defied the status quo throughout his career. From his early days in real estate to his tenure as the 45th President of the United States, Trump has demonstrated a willingness to go against the grain in pursuit of his objectives. In the realm of the real estate industry, he boldly constructed large, opulent buildings that deviated from the conventional high-rise apartments commonly seen in the city. Notably, he garnered attention by acquiring the commodore Hotel and transforming it into the renowned Grand Hyatt New York. Additionally, his creation of Trump Tower on Fifth Avenue solidified his position as a prominent figure, with the structure remaining an iconic symbol to this day.

Trump diverged from traditional political messaging and tactics, instead leveraging his charisma and celebrity status to connect with voters. His campaign strayed from the typical agenda by placing emphasis on overlooked issues such as immigration and trade, effectively challenging the status quo of mainstream politics. As President, Trump continued to disrupt the established order by implementing policies that were controversial and unconventional. Under his administration, an "America First" foreign policy was pursued (Beckwith, 2016), entailing the renegotiation of trade deals and a reduction in the United States' involvement in international organizations. Domestically, Trump championed tax reform, the construction of a border wall, and made efforts to repeal the Affordable Care Act. By bypassing traditional media outlets, he directly communicated with his supporters, generating controversy and dominating the news cycle through his use of tweets.

Employing aggressive tactics to gain leverage in negotiations and achieve desired outcomes.

- **Utilizing threats:** He employs various threats, such as the possibility of walking away from a deal, initiating legal action, or disclosing damaging information about the other party.

- **Intimidation tactics:** He may leverage his stature, wealth, or influence to intimidate the other party, leaving them with limited options but to acquiesce to his demands.

- **Strategic bluffing:** Trump is adept at employing bluffing techniques during negotiations. He might make audacious claims or demands that he knows are unlikely to be fulfilled, but he does so to gain an advantage in the negotiation process.

- **Insulting remarks:** He might resort to insulting the other party, targeting their intelligence or negotiation skills, with the intention of making them feel inferior.

- **Walking away or threatening to do so:** He may abruptly terminate ongoing negotiations or issue threats of doing so if his demands are not met.

- **Persisting with unfounded and extravagant assertions.** Former President Trump has gained notoriety for persisting with outlandish claims even when they lack credibility. One prominent instance is his assertion of winning the 2020 presidential election, despite the election results clearly indicating Joe Biden's decisive victory in both the popular vote and the Electoral College. Remarkably, he continues to assert this falsehood to this day. Another notable example is his claim that the COVID-19 pandemic was a hoax. Even when confronted with overwhelming evidence refuting his claims, he has shown reluctance to admit any wrongdoing or correct his statements. In response to media scrutiny, he often dismisses it as "fake news" or accuses it of being part of a biased establishment. It is evident that evidence or criticism does not sway Mr. Trump's unwavering commitment to his claims or alter his perception of the events in question.

Chapter IV
Is Donald Trump a real or a fake genius?

The question of whether Donald Trump is a real or a fake genius has sparked considerable debate and curiosity. To delve into this inquiry and gain a comprehensive understanding, it is crucial to conduct a thorough analysis and make comparisons between Trump's characteristic traits in both his public and professional life and the characteristic traits typically associated with a genius. In order to assess this, I will employ various measurements, including:

I. Identifying Trump's genius characteristic traits,
II. Studying his significant contributions in his respective field
III. Analyzing his methods and innovations
IV. Evaluating his overall impact and legacy.

By examining these elements, I will strive to shed light on the nature of Trump's intellectual abilities and ascertain whether they align with the qualities attributed to a real genius. Trump's legacy will be discussed in a separate chapter in the third section of this book.

I.Trump's genius characteristic traits

As stated previously, the most common and recognizable characteristic traits of a genius are: High levels of creativity, Intense focus and determination, exceptional intelligence, persistence and resilience, curiosity and thirst for knowledge, and being a risk taker.

Some of the ways in which Donald Trump's public and professional life could be seen as showcasing his creativity and his high levels of creativity are discussed below:

High intelligence

A. Marketing and Branding: Trump is known for his ability to brand and market himself effectively. He has been involved in various businesses over the years, including real estate, entertainment, and politics. In each of these areas, he has used his creativity to establish a strong brand and image for himself. He has given to his buildings and other properties distinctives names and designs to make them stand out and attract attention. Articles in the media have described trump as "Genius of self-promotion" and similar terms as far back as 2004 (ABC News, 2004). Trump has consistently been described to have exceptional self-promoting skills. Washington Post article headline describes him as "Donald Trump, the master of self-promotion in a 2015 article (Telnaes, 2015). In 2016 PBS published a piece on Trump with title "Meet young Donald Trump, a 'pioneer of self-promotion'.

B. Public Speaking: Trump is also known for his public speaking skills, which have often been described as entertaining and captivating. He has a knack for using language in creative ways to express his ideas and connect with his audience. He is also known for using repetition, humor, and rhetorical devices to make his points more memorable and impactful. These are evidence in the numerous speeches during his time as president of the United States, up until his speech on the 6th of January 2021 which has been said to incite violence that manifested in the Capitol riot.

C. Deal Making: Trump has a reputation for being a shrewd negotiator and dealmaker. He has been involved in many high-profile business deals over years, and his ability to find creative solutions to complex problems has been cited as key factor in his success. He is known for his willingness to take risks and his ability to think outside the box when it comes to finding solutions. The book "Trump: The Art of the Deal" by Donald Trump and Tony Schwartz a journalist, significantly contributed to building Trump's popularity as a businessman with reputation for deal making.

D. Social Media: Trump has also been very active on social media, particularly on twitter. He has used this platform to express his opinions and connect with his supporters in creative ways. He has been known to use humor, sarcasm, and provocative language to get his message across, and he has often been successful in generating a lot of attention and engagement with his tweets.

Curiosity and thirst for knowledge

The misbehavior displayed by Mr. Trump at home and in school could be interpreted as a reflection of his curiosity and thirst for knowledge. Given his advanced understanding and position ahead of his peers and the social system throughout his life, this curiosity might have manifested itself through aggression, arrogance, or defiance.

From an early age, he was heavily influenced by his father, a successful real estate developer, and displayed a strong eagerness to learn the intricacies of the industry (Karni and Rogers. 2021). Regardless of whether he was an avid reader or not, he actively sought out new information through alternative means. In his business career, Trump consistently demonstrated a willingness to explore new ideas and take risks, often seeking advice from experts across various fields. His tireless pursuit of knowledge and his remarkable ability to absorb and process vast amounts of data became well-known characteristics.

Even as a politician, Trump continued to exhibit curiosity and a thirst for knowledge. He became widely recognized for his unconventional approach to politics and his readiness to challenge the established norms. He fearlessly questioned existing practices, sought direct sources of information, and actively sought insights from advisors and experts In diverse fields.

Despite some controversial statements and actions directed towards advisors and experts, Trump also demonstrated a genuine interest in engaging with people from different backgrounds and perspectives. This showcased his openness to new ideas and his desire to learn from others. Trump's unwavering commitment to questioning, investigating, and challenging the unknown has been a defining aspect of his persona. The accomplishments of Trump administration listed in the white house archives included all-time lows in unemployment rates amongst African Americans, Asian Americans, Hispanic Americans, veterans, native Americans, people with disabilities and people with high school diploma. This shows his interest in impacting on diverse group of people.

Risk taker

Trump is well known for his flamboyant persona. As such, both his business ventures and professional career have been highly dominated and influenced by "Risk-taking behaviors". His business career provides ample examples of his risk-taking behavior. As a real estate developer, Trump took on ambitious projects that many others considered too risky. For example, in the early 1980s, he took over the commodore hotel in New York City, which was in dire financial straits. Rather than playing it safe and simply renovating the hotel, Trump embarked on an ambitious project to completely redevelop the site as the Grant Hyatt Hotel. The project required significant investment and involved navigating complex regulatory issues, but Trump's boldness and vision ultimately paid off: The Grand Hyatt Hotel became a major success and helped cement his reputation as a savvy businessman.

Intense focus and determination

Donald Trump has been known to work long hours and to be highly involved in the day-to-day operations of his businesses. He pays attention to details. He has been highly involved in the design and development of many of his own products and has been highly involved in the marketing and promotion of his businesses. His tenacity in the face of adversity once again proves his intense focus and determination to the area of his interest. For example, his ambition was to be the President of the United States: He first ran for president in 2000 as a candidate for the Reform Party, and he has been very vocal about his political beliefs and opinions on a wide range of issues. In

2016, he won the Republican Party's nomination and went on to win the election.

It is undeniable that Donald Trump is so intensely focused and determined that he has been criticized as being obsessive compulsive when engaged in his area of interest. He used to tweet intensely throughout the day, every day and any time. His twitter followers would wake up any time of the early morning and find his tweets. His high success in his diverse endeavors explains that Donald Trump has a remarkable level of focus and determination.

Exceptional intelligence

Intelligence is a complex and multi-faceted trait; therefore, it can be difficult to accurately measure or evaluate an individual's overall intelligence. In the case of Donald Trump, his "Exceptional Intelligence" can be measured or evaluated by his success in businesses acumen, marketing skills, political instincts, and negotiation skills.

A. Trump has been successful in real estates, hospitality, entertainment, and other industries, amassing a net of worth to be estimated to be billions of dollars. He has also written numerous books on business and management, including the "Art of the Deal', "Midas touch", "why we want you to be rich", "Think like a billionaire" and recently "Crippled America: how to make America great again". Many of his books have been best sellers. His post-presidency book, "Our Journey together" reportedly sold 20 million dollars as of Fberuary 2022 (Hartmann, 2022). Donald Trump's ability to identify and seize business opportunities, negotiate deals, and manage risks is a testament to his strategic thinking and financial acumen.

B. Marketing Skills: Trump has a natural talent for self-promotion and branding. He has made a name for himself as a celebrity and businessman throughout his appearances on reality TV show, his flamboyant style, and his controversial statements.

He masters the art of using social media to his advantage, using twitter to communicate directly with his supporters and rally them behind his causes.

C. Political instincts: Trump's success in the pollical arena is a testament to his ability to connect with voters and appeal to their emotions. He ran a successful campaign for the presidency in 2016, despite being a political outsider and facing intense opposition from the establishment. His populist message, anti-establishment rhetoric, and promises to bring back jobs and restore American greatness resonated with many Americans.

D. Trump has been known for his negotiation skills, honed through decades of deal-making in the business world. He has used his skills to his advantage in politics as well, as evidenced by his diplomatic efforts with North Korea and his negotiation of the USMCA (trade deal with Mexico and Canada).

Persistence and resilience

Resilience: Trump's ability to bounce back from setbacks and adversity is a testament to his resilience and mental toughness. Despite facing numerous legal and political challenges, including two impeachment trials and ongoing high-profile investigations, he has continued to remain a prominent figure in the public. In the 1990s, trump faced financial difficulties due to a series of bad investments, causing his businesses to lose hundreds of millions of dollars. He didn't give up; instead, he changed his strategy and filed for bankruptcy. He managed to turn his fortunes around by focusing on his real estate ventures. As an outsider in the pollical arena, he encountered numerous challenges from his campaign team to keep him online with the traditional way of campaigning, he maintained enough resistance and resilience to win the Republican Party nomination and defeat a professional politician Hilary Clinton in the general election.

Donald Trump's success in his public and professional life can largely be attributed to his resistance and resilience. Throughout his career, he has faced numerous obstacles and setbacks, but he has always managed to bounce back and continue pursuing his goals.

Despite facing criticism and backlash from the media and political opponents, he has remained steadfast in his beliefs and maintained a strong public persona. While some may disagree with his methods and approach, it cannot be denied that his resilience has played a significant role in his success.

II. Trump's significant contribution in his respective field.

In the early 1970'. Donald Trump joined his father's real estate development company and quickly rose through the ranks to become president of the company. He later went on to establish the Trump Organization, which includes a diverse range of businesses such as real estate, hotels, casinos, golf courses, and more. He has built a multi-billion-dollar empire that spans across the globe (Securities and Exchange Commission, 2005). Trump's businesses have been successful in creating jobs, generating revenue, and contributing to the growth of the economy.

Donald Trump has been a fixture on television and in popular culture for decades, with appearances on shows like The Apprentice and Saturday Night Live. Trump's celebrity status has helped to raise awareness of various social and political issues, and his outspoken nature has often made headlines. His contribution to the entertainment industry also extends to his ownership of the Miss Universe Organization, which produces the Miss Universe, Miss USA, and Miss Teen USA beauty pageants. Under his ownership, the pageants grew in popularity and generated significant revenue.

Donald Trump's most notable contribution has been in the field of politics. He has served as the 45th President of the United States from 2017 to 2021, after winning the presidential election as an outsider. His presidency was marked by a number of controversial policies and decisions, including his efforts to limit immigration, his response to the COVID-19 pandemic, and his foreign policy initiatives. His supporters credit him for his efforts to strengthen the economy, reduce unemployment, and promote American interest abroad. His administration implemented policies such as tax cuts, deregulation, and trade agreements that were aimed at boosting economy growth.

Donald Trump has made significant contributions in his respective fields of business, entertainment, and politics. As a successful entrepreneur, he has created jobs, generated revenue, and contributed to the growth of the economy. As a celebrity, he has raised awareness of various social and political issues, and as a politician, he has implemented policies aimed at promoting American interests.

Donald Trump has been on the Forbes 400 list for over 25 years and still remains on the list even after briefly dropping off in 2021 (Alexander, 2022). Donald Trump has also received two Emmys nominations as executive producer of the NBC show "The Apprentice" for the award of "outstanding reality-competition program". He also has a star on the Hollywood Walk of Fame. He has been awarded Person of the Year by Time and Financial Times in 2016 (Jackson, 2016).

III. Analyze Trump's methods and innovations.

To better grasp Donald Trump's high level of intelligent methods and innovation, a comprehensive analysis of his behavioral history during his tenure as the 45th President of the United States from 2017 to 2021 must be considered.

Donald Trump, as a well-known prolific twitter user, bypassed the filter of traditional social media outlets to reach out directly to millions of people and communicate his policy decisions, criticize his opponents, and rally his supporters.

Trump cultivated a strong personality cult among his supporters, often portraying himself as a strong leader who knows it all. He presented an "only me can fix it" approach portraying himself as the one who could solve America's problems. He demanded his supporters to be loyal to him personally, rather than to the Republican Party or conservative ideology.

Donald Trump rhetoric was often populist, which was appealing to the concerns of working-class Americans. He portrayed himself as a champion of the "forgotten man" and promised to fight against the Washington establishment.

Donald Trump's slogan political campaign was "Make America Great again" and his famous policy "America First" represented his vision for a return to a time when America was prosperous and powerful. He promised to revive the manufacturing industry, renegotiate trade deals, and bring back jobs to America.

"America First" slogan, used throughout his presidency, represented a nationalist and isolationist vision of American foreign policy. These slogans resonated with many of his supporters.

He implemented several policies: Tax cuts for businesses and individuals, deregulation, and renegotiation of trade deals. He also introduces tariffs on several goods imported from China and other countries. His immigration policy was focused on reducing illegal immigration and enhancing border security. He made entry to the US very hard for several Muslim-majority countries by placing travel ban on them. His policies led to the separation of families at the border. He also embarked on the construction of the border wall between US and Mexico.

Trump's presidency was often characterized as being driven by his personality and personal interest rather than policy goals. He frequently lashed out at critics on twitter, feuded with members of his own party, and made impulsive decisions that caught his own administration off guard. His administration often contradicted itself on key issues and frequently made false statements or misleading statements. They became very creative by initiation of "Alternative Facts", which is nothing but a pass to get out of trouble.

Donald Trump didn't have any problem to implement a policy for his famous use of executive orders, which allowed him to make policy decisions without the need for congressional approval. He signed a executive orders on a range of issue, including immigration, healthcare, and climate change.

Indeed, Donald Trump's methods and innovations during his presidency were often controversial and divisive. While some of his policies were popular among his supporters, others were criticized as being harmful to American interests and values. His use of social media platform, personality-driven politics, and populist rhetoric set him apart from previous presidents and made him a polarizing figure in American politics.

Overall, Trump's methods and innovations were controversial and divisive. While his supporters lauded his unconventional approach and willingness to shake up the political establishment, his opponents criticized his disregard for democratic norms and his divisive rhetoric. Regardless of one's opinion of his methods, it is undeniable that Trump's presidency had a significant impact on American politics and will continue to be the subject of intense debate for years to come.

Donald Trump is an innovative genius!

Donald Trump has met all the characteristic traits of a genius. From the early part of his life, he demonstrated he was very different from the members of his household. His siblings couldn't catch up with him, it seems, in everything/aspect in the house. Neither could the community schools. His parents couldn't either control or assist him with his higher demand needs. His parents had to look for expert's assistance, military school at age 13. Record showed that he excelled in the program (McAdams, 2020). Donald Trump's versatile and multi-task skills could have been misinterpreted as so-called 'misbehavior.' Donald Trump doesn't only excel in all his endeavors, but he revolutionizes and transformed all his fields of interest: Mentored by his father in real estate, he grew up to be a great real estate developer and soared to accomplish what his mentor and other notorious real-estate developers of his era had ever imagined doing.

Many would agree with me that Donald Trump revolutionized modern real estate by introducing innovative development models, leveraging technology to streamline processes, and redefining luxury standards, leaving an indelible mark on the industry. He is a polymath, given the way he masters the art of self-promoting, setting the tone for the social standard to his liking, and remaining a dominating American persona using social media platforms including television networks, entertainment, and twitter. He has crafted himself as a brand name just like so many other geniuses whose discoveries speak out for them. As a political outsider, Donald Trump has been shuffling the American politics to a point that it has never been (Shafer and Wagner, 2018). Despite his controversial political style, he outplayed 17 professional Republican candidates and one high profile Democratic nominee to win the Presidency of the United States. He said what other politicians have not been able to say, he ran away from the political establishment and set several records desirable or not with no consequences. Which other American citizen or other man or woman in the world has ever defeated The United States government of America so boldly and veraciously and not getting topped? No other one has done so adeptly and phenomenally as he has done it. He executed everything with such mastery that I'm convinced he possesses qualities that set him apart from the general population.

In the 2020 Presidential election, Joe Biden a lifetime politician, won 81,283,098 popular votes and Donald Trump, the outsider, won 74,222,958 popular votes. According to Pew Research Center, 66% of adult United States citizens voted (Igielnik, keeter and Hartig, 2021), more than 159 million Americans voted in 2020 election. That's the largest total voter turnout in U.S. history and the first time more than 140 million people voted. The election of 1876 holds the record for highest turnout: 82.6 percent. That, of course, was also one of America's most controversial and consequential elections. Donald Trump has initiated major challenges to the 246-year-old American Democracy, which consequences will take years to be seen. Donald Trump has brought more people to watch TV, read the news, and involved in the daily occurrences of the American politics. He has unveiled the American hypocrisy by revealing or exposing some of the covert behaviors that the American government has been orchestrated around the world. He openly criticized the American institutions, praising foreign leaders, and dismissed American intelligence and embraced the foreigners. That is an eye opening for the world and empowerment for certain American citizens to think out of the box and de-camouflage the so-called 'freedom of speech.'

Comparing Donald Trump's life to those of some prominent geniuses and using a thorough analysis of what it takes to be a genius, I am convinced to concur with Donald Trump that he is a fine genius for he has exhibited most characteristic traits of being a genius and just like many other geniuses, Donald Trump is endowed with high intelligence and drive to transform or re-innovate. Which has been demonstrated throughout his demeanor, behaviors, and achievements. Donald Trump's legacy as a genius will take few years yet to be fully developed. However, with certainty the following election will give birth to some candidates applying the Trumpisms' way of campaigning or administering.

In conclusion, when analyzing Donald Trump's methods and innovations, it becomes evident that he possessed a unique combination of characteristics and skills that contributed to his success in various fields. Trump's risk-taking attitude, determination, excellent negotiation skills, and ability to spot opportunities set him apart as a real genius in his own right. His effective communication and branding strategies further enhanced his influence and enabled him to build a successful career in real estate, entertainment, and ultimately, politics. Additionally, his ability to surround himself with competent individuals and make tough decisions when needed further solidified his reputation as a shrewd and capable leader. Despite the controversies and criticisms, Donald Trump's impact and legacy will undoubtedly be debated for years to come, highlighting the undeniable mark of a true genius in his field of interest.

Section 2
The Untouchable Champion

Donald Trump is not only a genius, but an untouchable champion! This section of the book analyses how Donald Trump has proven himself a champion. We also look at Donald Trump's biggest opponent yet, The Unite States legal system, and count the wins and losses of both sides.

Chapter V
What makes one a champion?

A champion is someone who has achieved the highest level of success in their field. Whether it's in sports, business, or the arts, champions possess a winning attitude that drives them to excel. While talent and skill are certainly important, it is a champion's mindset that sets them apart from the competition. Few examples of champions highlight their unwavering dedication and relentless pursuit of greatness. Consider the legendary basketball player Michael Jordan, whose relentless work ethic and competitive spirit propelled him to six NBA championships. Similarly, Serena Williams, a dominant force in tennis, has shown remarkable resilience and mental toughness, consistently pushing herself to the limit and capturing numerous Grand Slam titles. In the world of business, we find visionary leaders like Elon Musk, who revolutionized the electric car industry through his innovative thinking and determination. These individuals demonstrate that being a champion entail more than just talent; it involves a deep commitment, unwavering focus, and an unyielding belief in oneself.

Donald Trump's mindset distinguishes him as a champion.

The concept of TRP was recently proposed and this is applied here to present an understanding of Donald Trump's champion mindset. "Success is not just a coincidence; it's about cultivating a winning cocktail mindset, known as the Tenacity, Resiliency, and Perseverance (TRP) shot. Blend unwavering determination, bounce back from setbacks, and embark on a relentless pursuit of your goals, and you'll find yourself savoring the sweet taste of victory." - Jumel Pluviose © 2023.

Tenacity, resiliency, and perseverance, when these personality traits are combined or synchronized, they can play a major role in an individual's personal and professional growth. They are three essential qualities that can be used as a real weapon to help individuals overcoming challenges, achieving their goals, and groundbreaking. Tenacity, Resiliency, and Perseverance (TRP) can further be considered as a recipe for winning (TRP = Winning Cocktail Mindset = TRP shot). I was fortunate to witness firsthand the indomitable spirit of my mother Jeanne D. Osias as she embraced an unwavering mindset, surmounting insurmountable odds to ensure the well-being of herself and our family. In the face of seemingly impossible circumstances, my mother exemplified tenacity, resilience and determination, crafting a path towards securing the most fundamental necessities. Her unwavering attitude serves as a testament to the incredible power of the human spirit to overcome any challenge that comes ahead.

It seems to me that the winning cocktail mindset is Mr. Trump's most dominant innate instinct and strength. It is my intuition, understanding, and belief that Mr. Trump is fully aware of the magical use of the TRP shot. As such, for each breath taken he is consciously using it.

Tenacity refers to the ability to persist in the face of challenges or obstacles. Tougher the challenges get more tenacious the person become. Resilience is the ability to bounce back from setbacks and to maintain a positive outlook despite adversity. Perseverance is the determination to keep going even when progress is slow, or success seems distant.

Donald Trump is tenacious in the way he has demonstrated throughout his life the ability to persist in the face of challenges or obstacles, and the ease and thrill to get tough on his opponents. He is resilient by mastering the ability to bounce back from setbacks and maintain a positive outlook despite adversity. Regardless of what the outcome is, Donald Trump demonstrated the determination to keep going even when progress is slow, loss is imminent, or success seems distant or even impossible. These three characteristic traits (tenacity, resiliency, and perseverance) of Donald Trump have been critical to his success as a businessman and politician. They have also built him up to develop a strong mindset and overcome the inevitable setbacks and failures that have arisen in the path to his success. This winning cocktail mindset has distinguished him as a champion.

Donald Trump is widely regarded as one of the successful businesspeople and politicians in recent history. It appeared to me that the key to his success is that throughout his career, he has relied heavily on his tenacity, resiliency, and perseverance as key strength and strategies to achieve success. In his early years, Donald Trump inherited a small real estate development from his father. He worked hard to expand it into a large and successful and worldwide business. Along the way, he faced financial difficulties, legal challenges, and intense competition. However, he persevered through these obstacles and continued to work tirelessly to grow his business empire. He has been relentless in his pursuit of success, refusing to give up even when facing seemingly insurmountable challenges. For example, when he faced bankruptcy in the early 1990s (American Bankruptcy Institute), he refused to let the setback define him and instead he worked tirelessly to rebuild his business empire. He could only keep trying because of his tenacious strength. In addition to his tenacity, Trump has also shown remarkable resiliency in the face of adversity. He has weathered countless storms throughout his career, including lawsuits, financial difficulties, and political scandals. However, he has always bounced back stronger than before, demonstrating a remarkable ability to adapt and overcome obstacles.

Finally, Donald Trump's perseverance has been a key factor in his success in both business and politics. He has never been one to shy away from a challenge or give up in the face of adversity. Instead, he is determined and committed to his goals even when others considered it impossible or crazy. Donald Trump's life comprises of conflicts, challenges, and calculated or uncalculated battles; he adapts, adjusts, finds alternative/situational strategies as needed, while he still maintains a sense of purpose and dedication to the goal.

Undoubtedly, Donald Trump's remarkable achievements in both business and politics can be primarily attributed to his unparalleled tenacity, resiliency, and unwavering perseverance, which form the very essence of his Winning Cocktail Mindset or TRP shot. Throughout his journey, he has consistently demonstrated an unyielding determination to overcome countless obstacles and emerge triumphant in the face of adversity. Regardless of the nature or magnitude of setbacks, Trump's fearlessness stems from his innate DNA, consisting of the powerful concoction that is his Winning Cocktail Mindset. It is this unique blend that has propelled him to unparalleled heights of success.

Chapter VI
The Intersection of Family Influence, Education, and Strategic Maneuvering in Donald J. Trump's Journey to Success

Donald J. Trump is Donald J. Trump

From the very outset of his life, Donald Trump recognized that he couldn't fully realize and develop his potential by simply conforming to the norms, rules, and laws that govern the behavior of ordinary individuals. Whether consciously or unconsciously, Trump embarked on a path where he pursued his own desires and aspirations, positioning himself as a challenger to the prevailing status quo, rules, and regulations. He quickly grasped the understanding that to lead a purposeful and impactful life, he needed to skillfully navigate the obstacles imposed by laws, societal conventions, and established boundaries. Few individuals comprehend this principle as well as Donald J. Trump. he understands that living a purpose-driven life necessitates mastering the art of overcoming inevitable roadblocks.

During his early childhood, Donald Trump was known for his "misbehavior," which can be understood as his tendency to challenge established rules within his family and school. He disrupted the daily operations of these institutions, often making authority figures uncomfortable with his constant and unconventional questions and actions, which pushed boundaries and forced others to think outside the box or step out of their comfort zones. As a result, Trump was eventually expelled from community schools and sent to a boarding school (Schwartzman and Miller, 2016), where it was hoped that he could be controlled, disciplined, or conditioned to become a well-mannered citizen. In his book (Donald Trump, 1987), Trump discusses his undergraduate career by saying that he also considered going to film school after he graduated from the New York Military Academy but ended up choosing the family real estate business.

As gifted as Donald Trump, formally or informally, he was coached or mentored by his dad, Fred Trump in business dealings. In the late 1920s, Fred Trump began his construction business by building single-family homes in the Queens and Brooklyn boroughs of New York City. From the late 1940s to the late 1950s, he built thousands of residential units, primarily located in Brooklyn, with the help of a federal loan guaranteed to encourage the construction of affordable housing throughout. He also worked for the forces by building federally subsidized housing in Virginia and Pennsylvania for military personnel and shipyard workers during WWII. In 1954, the Senate Banking Committee investigated Fred for exploiting the loan-guarantee scheme by overestimating the price of his construction projects to secure larger loans from financial institutions and retain the disparity between the amount of credit and his actual construction costs. Fred acknowledged to a Senate committee in 1954 that the Beach Haven apartment complex in Brooklyn was built for $3.7 million less than the amount of his government-insured loan. Although he was never charged with a criminal offence, he could not receive government loan guarantees after that. As per a New York state investigation a decade later, Fred used the profit from a state-insured loan agreement to build a shopping mall that was his property. He could not obtain state financial assistance for residential constructions in Brooklyn's Coney Island neighborhood after repaying $1.2 million to the state.

Donald J Trump became more conscious of power and privileges.

Between 1959 to 1964, Donald Trump joined New York Military Academy, Fordham University in the Bronx from 1964 to 1966, and the University of Pennsylvania's Wharton School of Finance and Commerce from 1966 to 1968, where he earned a Bachelor of Science degree in economics. He acquired a diagnosis of bone spurs in 1968, during the Vietnam War, which qualified him for a medical exemption from the military draught. He already earlier had received four draught deferments for education. Trump worked full-time for his father's company, assisting him in managing the company's rental housing assets, which were estimated to be between 10,000 and 22,000 units at the time of his graduation. In 1974, he was appointed president of the Trump Organization, which consists of Trump-owned businesses and partnerships.

Throughout the 1960s and early 1970s, several accusations of ethnic and racial discrimination against African Americans and other minority groups were filed against Trump-owned housing developments in New York City, Cincinnati, Ohio, and Norfolk, Virginia (Howard T, Civil Rights Litigation Clearinghouse, 2016).In 1973, Fred and Donald Trump, as well as their corporation, were sued by The U.S. Department of Justice for allegedly breaching the Fair Housing Act (1968) in the operation of 39 apartment buildings in New York City. The Trumps initially sued the Justice Department for $100 million, alleging their reputations had been injured. The settlement was reached two years later in a method that did not affect Trump to admit guilt. Donald Trump significantly expanded his father's business by investing in luxury hotels and residential complexes and changing its geographic emphasis to Manhattan and then to Atlantic City, New Jersey, in the late 1970s and 1980s. He did it due to the help of his father's loans, gifts, and other financial aid, as well as his father's political ties in New York City. In 1976, he bought the run-down Commodore Hotel near Grand Central Station under a complex profit-sharing agreement with the city that included a 40-year property tax exemption historically significant in New York City. Trump restored the property and relaunched it in 1980 as the 1,400-room Grand Hyatt Hotel. He relied on a construction credit secured by the Hyatt Corporation, which became a partner in the project and his father. In 1983, Trump Tower debuted it as an office, retail, and residential complex in conjunction with the Equitable Life Assurance Company. Trump's Manhattan condominium and the Trump Organization's headquarters were eventually housed on 56th Street and Fifth Avenue in the 58-story structure. Significant Manhattan properties established by Trump throughout the 1980s include the Trump Plaza residential cooperative

(1984), the Trump Parc luxury condominium complex (1986), and the 19-story Plaza Hotel (1988), a heritage structure for which Trump invested over $400 million.

In conclusion, Donald J. Trump's journey to success and prominence can be attributed to a combination of factors that shaped and groomed him for a life of influence and power. From his early days challenging established rules within his family and school, Trump displayed a determination to push boundaries and question the status quo. This mindset was further honed during his time at the New York Military Academy, where he learned discipline, leadership, and the value of strategic maneuvering.

However, one cannot overlook the significant impact of family influence on Trump's development. Mentored by his father, Fred Trump, in the intricacies of the real estate business, Donald Trump gained invaluable insights and guidance that allowed him to navigate complex business dealings and seize lucrative opportunities. Fred's experiences, both positive and controversial, served as a blueprint for Trump to understand the intricacies of the legal system and exploit loopholes to his advantage.

Furthermore, Trump's educational background, including his time at the University of Pennsylvania's Wharton School of Finance and Commerce, equipped him with the knowledge and skills necessary for financial success. Combined with his father's financial support, Trump leveraged these resources to expand his empire, strategically investing in luxury hotels and residential complexes, particularly in Manhattan and Atlantic City. Through it all, Donald J. Trump demonstrated an innate ability to overcome obstacles and use his family influence, education, and understanding of the legal system to his advantage. His determination to challenge norms and pursues his own desires has shaped his career and fueled his rise to prominence.

While opinions may differ on the impact and consequences of Trump's actions, one cannot deny that he embodies the spirit of an individual who has learned to master the art of overcoming roadblocks in pursuit of his goals. Whether you admire or criticize his methods, Donald J. Trump's journey is a testament to the power of family influence, education, and a strategic approach to navigating the business and legal landscape.

Chapter VII
Donald Trump triumphs through adversities

In the realm of adversities, challenges, and a curiosity to cross boundaries, Donald Trump has emerged as a testament to resilience and triumph. Throughout his life, Trump has embraced these driving forces as catalysts for progress, defying conventional norms and pursuing paths less traveled. Analyzing his life convinces me to believe that "if a task were effortless, it simply wasn't Donald Trump's doing." Undeterred by the energy expended and the relentless scrutiny faced, Trump has forged ahead, achieving remarkable success in both the business and political spheres. His indomitable spirit and ability to overcome obstacles have not only shaped his own journey but have left an indelible mark on the fabric of our society. By delving into the remarkable tale of Donald Trump's triumphs, we gain a profound understanding of the power of determination and the heights that can be reached in the face of adversity.

In the 1990s, Trump has faced significant financial difficulties, leading to several bankruptcies and the loss of some of his assets. Despite those setbacks, Trump continue to pursue new ventures and eventually regained his financial footing. For example, Trump's first major bankruptcy was the Trump Taj Mahal, a lavish casino in Atlantic City (Lipson, 2016). The project was initially supposed to cost $1 billion but ended up costing nearly $1.2 billion. The casino struggled to turn a profit and filed for bankruptcy in 1991, just a year after it opened.

Another one of the Trump's Atlantic City casinos, the Trump Plaza, filed for bankruptcy the following year in 1992. The casino was burdened with debt and was struggling to compete with newer and more popular casinos in the area. Trump's casino business continued to struggle in the 2000s, and 2004, Trump's Hotels and Casino Resorts filed for bankruptcy. The company amassed more than $1.8 billion in debt, and trump stepped down as the company's CEO as part of the restructuring process.

Trump's Casino business faced more financial difficulties during the Great Recession, and in 2009, Trump Entertainment Resorts filed for bankruptcy. The company was burdened with more than $1.2 billion in debt and was unable to keep up with its interest payments. One challenge after another one, in 2014, Trump's Entertainment Resort had to file for bankruptcy again for the company struggling with competition and finding a buyer (American Bankruptcy Institute).

Despite the setbacks caused by his bankruptcies, Donald Trump managed to recover and rebuild his business empire stronger over the years. Here are some ways in which he bounced back:

Following the bankruptcy of his casino business, Trump shifted his focus back to real estate's development. He embarked on several high-profile projects in cities such as Chicago and Las Vegas, including the Trump International Hotel and Tower in Chicago and the Trump International Hotel Las Vegas.

In 2004, Trump became the host of the reality TV show 'The Apprentice', which became a massive hit and cemented his status as a media personality. The show ran for 14 seasons and gave Trump a new platform to promote his business ventures and brand.

Trump has also leveraged his name and brand through licensing deals, which allow other companies to use his name and image in exchange for royalties. He has licensed his name to a wide range of products and services, including clothing, home décor, and even a line of steaks.

Ultimately, Donald Trump's journey culminated in his historic run for the presidency of the United States in 2016. Against all odds, he secured victory, becoming the 45th President of the country. This achievement showcases not only his resilience in overcoming personal adversities but also his ability to resonate with a significant portion of the American population.

In conclusion, Donald Trump's triumphs through adversities exemplify the power of determination and resilience. Despite facing financial setbacks and enduring relentless scrutiny, he managed to rebuild his business empire, solidify his brand, and ultimately ascend to the highest office in the nation. His unwavering spirit and ability to overcome obstacles have left an indelible mark on the fabric of our society, forever reminding us that triumph can be found even in the most challenging circumstances. Donald Trump's life stands as a testament to the fact that true champions are forged through adversity.

Chapter VIII
Donald Trump's readiness, confidence, determination to be the all-time champion.

Donald Trump's grooming equipped him to excel in all areas of his interest. Indeed, he faced numerous lawsuits throughout his career. From allegations of fraud and defamation to sexual misconduct, these legal battles have tested his ability to navigate through challenging circumstances. Yet, time and again, Trump has demonstrated his knack for overcoming legal challenges and finding ways to emerge unscathed. Here is a brief overview of some of the lawsuits and strategies employed by Trump and his legal team to overcome them:

Lawsuits

In 2013, New York Attorney General Eric Schneiderman sued Trump for $40 million, alleging that Trump University was a fraudulent enterprise. Trump's legal team argued that the lawsuit was politically motivated, and that Trump University had provided valuable education to its students. However, in November 2016, Trump agreed to pay $25 million to settle the lawsuits.

In 2016, Donald Trump settled a lawsuit brought by former students at Trump University for $25million (Office of New York State Artoney General, April 9, 2018). The students alleged that they were defrauded by the real estate school, which promised to teach them the secrets of Trump's success but failed to deliver. Trump's legal team could have tried to argue that the students were aware of the risks and made the decision to enroll voluntarily. However, settling the case may have been a strategic move to avoid negative publicity during the presidential campaign.

In 2016, former" Apprentice" contestant Summer Zervos sued Trump for defamation after he called her allegations of sexual assault false. Trump's legal team argued that he was immune from the lawsuit because he was president, but a New York judge ruled in March 2018 that the lawsuit could proceed. In October 2020, a New York appeals court rejected Trump's request to dismiss the lawsuit, allowing it to proceed.

In 2017, a group of Democrat lawmakers sued Trump for violating the Emoluments Clause of the constitution, which prohibits presidents from receiving gifts or payments from foreign governments. Trump's legal team argued that the lawsuits were politically motivated, and that Emoluments Clause did not apply to him and that he has divested from his businesses to avoid conflicts of interest. However, in March 2021, a federal appeals court allowed the lawsuit to proceed.

In 2018, adult film actress Stormy Daniels sued Trump for defamation after he claimed that she was lying about their alleged affair. Trump's legal team argued that he was protected by the First Amendment and that the claims were not defamatory because they were made in the context of a political campaign. However, a Federal judge ordered Daniels to pay Donald Trump $293,000 in legal fees ((Drenon, 2023).

In 2019, wrier E. Jean Carroll accused Trump of sexually assaulting her in the 1990s. Trump denied the allegations and claimed that Carroll was lying. Carroll sued Trump for defamation, but Trump's legal team argued that he was immune from the lawsuit because he made the allegedly defamatory comments while he was president. However, in March 2021, the US Supreme Court allowed the lawsuit to proceed.

In 2020, Dominion Voting Systems sued Trump, his campaign, and several of his allies for defamation after they falsely claimed that Dominion's Voting machines were rigged to steal the election. Trump's legal team argued that he was protected by the First Amendment and that the claims were not defamatory because they were made in the context of a political campaign. However, in August 2021, Dominion filed a $1.6 billion lawsuit against Fox News, alleging that the network had also spread false claims about Dominion's voting machines.

In 2020, Deutsche Bank, one of Trump's lenders, sued him for defaulting on a $340 million loan. Trump's legal team argued that the lawsuit was politically motivated and that Deutsche Bank had previously agreed to restructure the loan. However, in January 2021, a New York judge ruled that the lawsuit could proceed.

In 2020, Mary Trump, Donald Trump's niece sued him and his siblings for fraud, claiming that they cheated her out of her share of the family's inheritance. Trump's legal team argued that the lawsuit was meritless, and that Mary Trump was bound by a confidentially agreement signed in 2001. However, in February 2021, a New York judge ruled that the lawsuit could proceed.

Following the January 6, 2021, riot at the US Capital, Trump faced multiple lawsuits from individuals and organizations who claimed that he incited the violence. Trump's legal team argued that he was protected by the First Amendment and that his comments did not directly incite violence. However, in February 2021, the U.S. Senate voted to impeach Trump for incitement of insurrection.

Trump's legal team employed various strategies, to overcome them, including arguing that the lawsuits were politically motivated, that the allegations were false or baseless, Trump was protected by the First Amendment, and that he was immune from certain types of lawsuits because he was the president. However, the outcomes of these lawsuits varied, some cases resulted in Trump being ordered to pay damages or legal fees, some were settlements or judgments against Trump, and others still ongoing.

Impeachments

Donald Trump, the 45th President of the United States, was impeached twice during his tenure in office. In December 2019, Donald Trump was impeached for the first time before completing his first two years in office (Bausum, 2021). The House of Representatives voted to impeach Trump on two accounts: abuse of power and obstruction of Congress. The impeachment was related to allegations that Trump had pressured the President of Ukraine to investigate his political rival, Joe Biden, and his son, Hunter Biden in exchanged to military aid (116th Congress (2019-2020) H.Res.755).

Donald Trump and his legal team adopted a strategy of attacking the process and the legitimacy of the impeachment inquiry. They argued that the impeachment was a partisan attack on the President and that he had done nothing wrong. They also argued that the President had the right to conduct foreign policy as he saw fit. Trump's legal team also criticized the evidence presented by the house and argued that the President had not committed any impeachable offenses.

Outcome: The Senate acquitted Trump of both charges in February 2020.

In January 2021, two years after the first impeachment and few days exactly before he left the office, The Representatives of the house impeached Mr. Trump for the second time. The impeachment was related to allegations that Trump incited a mob of his supporters to storm the U>S. Capitol on January 6th, 2021, in an attempt to overturn the results of the 2020 Presidential election (117th Congress (2021-2022) H.Res. 24).

Trump's legal team argued that the impeachment was politically motivated and that the impeachment politically motivated and that the President had done nothing wrong. They also argued that the impeachment was unconstitutional, as the President already left office. Trump's legal team also criticized the evidence presented by the house and argued that the President had not incited the violence that occurred at the capito Outcome: in February 2021, the Senate acquitted Trump of the charges.

Grand jury investigations

As Donald Trump was swearing into office, a grand jury investigation was set up due to mystery surrounding his campaign, Mueller investigation. Robert Mueller, the special counsel appointed to investigate Russian interference in 2016 US presidential election, conducted a grand jury investigation into possible collusion between the Trump campaign and Russian officials. The investigation also looked into potential obstruction of justice by the President.

Trump's legal team claimed that the investigation was politically motivated, and that Mueller had exceeded his authority. They also argued that there was no obstruction of justice because Trump was acting within his constitutional powers as president.
The investigation concluded in March 2019, and Mueller's report found no evidence of collusion but did not exonerate Trump as acting within his constitutional powers as president.

In 2021, the New York State Attorney General's office and the Manhattan District Attorney's office were investigating the Trump Organization for possible financial crimes, including tax fraud and insurance fraud. The office impaneled a grand jury in March 2021. The New York State Attorney General's office is also conducting a civil investigation into similar allegations.

Trump's legal team has called the investigations politically motivated and has argued that the prosecutors are biased against him. They have also argued that the investigations are a violation of his constitutional rights and have challenged the legality of subpoenas issued by the grand jury. In August 2021, a grand Jury indicted the Trump Organization and its CFO (Chief Financial Officer) on charges of tax fraud and other crimes.

Georgia election interference: In February 2021, a grand jury was impaneled in Fulton County, Georgia to investigate allegations of election interference by Trump and others in connection with the 2020 presidential election.

Trump's legal team has denied any wrongdoing and has argued that the investigation is politically motivated. They also questioned the authority of the grand jury and the legitimacy of the investigation.

Despite facing an array of lawsuits spanning different areas, Donald Trump has proven himself adept at finding legal solutions and strategies to overcome the challenges thrown his way. Through his tenure as a business tycoon and his controversial presidency, Trump has exhibited resilience in the face of legal adversity. Whether it was his ability to build a strong legal defense, leverage settlements, or employ persuasive tactics, he has managed to navigate through various legal battles successfully. As the legacy of Donald Trump continues to be debated, his legal prowess and ability to overcome lawsuits will undoubtedly be an enduring aspect of his narrative.

Chapter IX
Donald Trump fights like an innate champion.

One may wonder where Donald Trump finds the energy, drive, strength, and resilience to fight all those everlasting battles furiously from the beginning of his life (childhood) till this day (geriatric). Nothing has stopped him from moving forward his agenda. He acquired tremendous knowledge and experience in the battlefield against all types or sort of adversaries, competitors, or enemies. Weather Donald Trump's enemies are weak or powerful, petty or serious, a candidate or the deep state, he uses all his arsenal to fight it. I believe that Trump doesn't approach an opponent based on its size, strength, or look; either underestimates his opponent because of its capacity or prior successful histories. Donald Trump has mastered the art of winning and understood early on to remain a champion, he must continuously use the same tactics at all levels whether it's in junior, college, or professional, which is to attack any so-opponent seriously and furiously.

At the Junior phase, Donald Trump defeated his siblings at home. his classmates at elementary school couldn't catch up with him either. He was a different breed that required special and advanced accommodation for his needs. It's said that 'It takes the whole community to raise a child'. So was in the case of Donald J Trump. His 'misbehavior' has proven that Donald J Trump didn't belong to regular school system. For this reason, at 13 years old, Donald Trump needed to fast track the system to suit his academic needs. The most suitable environment for him at that time was the New York Military Academy. Where at 17 he was named captain of his senior year (Miller, 2016).

Critical knowledge transfer from Father Trump to son Trump.

During his time in college, Donald Trump embarked on a professional journey alongside his father, Fred, gaining invaluable insights into the world of work. Throughout his college years, he had the opportunity to observe and learn from his father about effectively navigating the bureaucratic landscape, including engaging with government officials to achieve his objectives, acquiring desired favors, and resolving legal matters in case they reached trial and were not favorable. Leveraging his father's political connections, he managed to obtain five draft deferments from the Vietnam War (Shane III, 2019). Subsequently, he ventured into contract dealings with the government, establishing connections with governmental officials, and assembling a team of skilled experts to aid him in various matters.

Donald Trump's remarkable factors to being a rock champ:

Donald Trump was born in 1946. Between 1959 to 1964, Donald Trump joined New York Military Academy, Fordham University in the Bronx from 1964 to 1966, and the University of Pennsylvania's Wharton School of Finance and Commerce from 1966 to 1968, where he earned a Bachelor of Science degree in economics. He acquired a diagnosis of bone spurs in 1968, during the Vietnam War, which qualified him for a medical exemption from the military draught (Shane III, 2019). He already earlier had received four draught deferments for education.

Trump worked full-time for his father's company, assisting him in managing the company's rental housing assets, which were estimated to be between 10,000 and 22,000 units at the time of his graduation. In 1974, he was appointed president of the Trump Organization, which consists of Trump-owned businesses and partnerships. Throughout the 1960s and early 1970s, several accusations of ethnic and racial discrimination against African Americans and other minority groups were filed against Trump-owned housing developments in New York City, Cincinnati, Ohio, and Norfolk,

Virginia. In 1973, Fred and Donald Trump, as well as their corporation, were sued by The U.S. Department of Justice for allegedly breaching the Fair Housing Act (1968) in the operation of 39 apartment buildings in New York City (Reuters Fact Check, 2021). The Trumps initially sued the Justice Department for $100 million, alleging their reputations had been injured. The settlement was reached two years later in a method that did not affect Trump to admit guilt.

This moment was the most valuable and meaningful for Donald Trump given the fact that he has applied his knowledge, critical thinking, and his winning mindset cocktail in a larger and higher scale. His 'misbehavior' was aimed directly at the general population (breaching the Fair Housing Act (1968)) and the U.S. government). The settlement was reached two years later in a method that did not affect Trump to admit guilt.

It seems to me as if by age 24 (1946 - 1970), Donald Trump was equipped with all schooling and mentorship needed to fly on his own to be the untouchable champion. Be it college or university, undergrad or postgrad, and magnum cum laude or Nobel Price, Donald Trump earned his degree and more importantly the knowledge of the U.S. Justice system and the confidence that builds up his ego and belief that he can defeat enemies, change the system, and submerge above the law regardless of the inflations or circumstances.

At the professional phase, Donald Trump was only cruising boldly and fearlessly since he already acquired knowledge and experience to play the game to be the untouchable champion. Same way Donald Trump set standard in the business and entertainment industry, he also set his own rules in politics. It is my understanding and belief that Donald Trump's victory consists of him winning the case, being compensated for suing or being sued, having allegations against him being dismissed or settled at a low cost if judgement is not favorable to him. His rules are many and numerous which could be summarized in one sentence: If he is not the winner, the election must have been rigged.

Now that the rules of the game are clear, Donald Trump is set and ready to make history, set records, and leave a legacy after his name. His main opponent is the deep states and anyone or anything else that might constitute a barrier to his objectives. As an American businessman, as controversial as Donald Trump is, he has lived a wonderful career and left his imprint in all the fields of his interest. Be it construction, entertainment or politics, he has set remarkable standards to look up to and be proud of. At the expense of his success and persona, he had engaged in multiple, unusual, and ongoing battles against the Deep State.

Those everlasting, ongoing, and unprecedented battles have shaken the American society to an extent that it has never been shaken before, and they raised the world's attention to certain issues once overlooked. Leaving everyone wondering what the HECK is going on. This Haitian proverb: 'Pia poul la craze zay' translated to 'The chicken's leg broke its own egg' said it all.

I wondered what this Haitian metaphor looks like to you. Sure, you might have a different or better way of expressing it. I would love to hear your point of view. Here is mine: The whole 'thingy' looks to me as if it's the case of a student defeating his/her teacher; a mentee outsmarting his/her mentor; a duper has been duped; and or it takes a piece of diamond to cut another piece of diamond. I also see it as a soccer, tennis, basketball, baseball, or boxing game with two teams competing, spectators, and commentator. I guessed you guessed that I am your commentator, didn't you? Let's do it!
Ready?
Go!
If we miss, reset and go!

Chapter X
Donald J Trump VS the deep state

Who is Donald Trump? And who is the Deep State?

Donald Trump is out of presentation. He was born a genius though labeled 'misbehavior', a Catalyst American who is hungry to write a new page in the American history book after 222 years of so-called independence, and a political outsider who bypasses the American hypocrisy to express his mind blatantly even if it's about an alternative true. By far, Donald Trump has been the only one man in history who has been defeating the U.S. Empire in all imaginable battle fields openly and has not yet stood up, not even for a preliminary interview. Readers, spectators, and fans, the untouchable champion, Donald J Trump!!!

Who is the Deep State?

To really understand the Deep State, a brief summary of its birth needs to be brought up to light. England established its first colony in what is now the United States in 1607, with the founding of Jamestown, Virginia (Library of Congress: Presentation US History Primary Source Timeline). Over the next several decades, England established several additional colonies along the eastern coast of North America, including Massachusetts, New York, Virginia. These colonies were primarily established for economic reasons, with the English seeking to expand their trade and increase their wealth. The colonies produced valuables resources such as tobacco, sugar, and lumber, which were in high demand in Europe. To ensure that these resources, were available for English use, the British government established a system of trade policies known as Mercantilism. Under this system, the colonies were required to export their goods to England and purchase England goods in return. This created a profitable trade relationship for England but placed significant restrictions on the economic development of the colonies.

Over time, tensions grew between the colonies and the government, as the colonists sought greater economic and political independence. Years of pollical tensions and colonial rebellion led to protests of unjust and oppressive British taxation policies by many colonies. In response to these protests, the British government attempted to assert its authority over the colonies, leading to armed conflicts such as the Boston Massacre and the battles of Lexington and Concord. These events fueled calls for independence among colonies, and in 1775 the Continental Congress established a Continental Army to fight for their cause. Several years of tensions eventually led to the American Revolution and the establishment of the United States as an independent nation. On July 4th, 1776, the United States of America declared its independence from Great Britain.

After several years of negotiations, the Treaty of Paris was signed in 1783, formally recognizing the United States as an independent nation and establishing the boundaries of its territory. This event marked the birth of the United Stated of America and set the stage for the country's rapid growth and emergence as a global superpower.

The United States of America's rise to becoming a superpower can be traced back to its birth as an independent nation in 1776. With a vast landmass, abundant natural resources, and a rapidly growing population, the country quickly became an economic powerhouse. Throughout the 19th century, the US expanded its territory and became a dominant force in international trade (US Department of States, Office of the Historian).

The country's role as a superpower was solidified in the aftermath of World War II, when the US emerged as one of the few major powers not devasted by the conflict. Through its leadership in the post-war era, the US became the dominant military and economic power in the world, playing a key role in the creation of the United Nations and establishing global institutions such as the international Monetary fund and the world bank (World bank Archives).

Throughout the latter half of the 20th century, the US was involved in numerous conflicts around the world, including the Korean War, Vietnam War, and Gulf War. The country's military might be coupled with a booming economy and technological advancements, leading to a period of unparalleled prosperity known as the post-World War II economic boom (Vonyo, 2008). In recent years, the US has faced challenges to its superpower status, including economic competition from emerging markets such as China, as well as political and social divisions within the country itself. Despite those challenges, The US remains a dominant force in global politics and economics, and its influence is felt around the world.

The United States of America has a Hierarchical system of power that involves three main levels; the state level, the federal level, and what some refer to as the "Deep State." At the state level, each of the 50 states has its own government and is responsible for governing itself according to its own laws and constitution. This including managing issues related to education, public safety, transportation, and more state affairs.

At the federal level, the central government is responsible for issues that affect the entire country. This includes managing foreign policy, national defense, and monetary policy, as well as regulating interstate commerce and enforcing federal laws.

The concept of the "deep state" is more controversial and refers to the idea that there are hidden, unelected bureaucrats and officials who hold significant power and influence within the federal government. Some people believe these individuals operate outside of the normal channels of government and can exert undue influence on policy decisions. However, this concept is not widely accepted by mainstream political scientists or government officials.

The United States or deep state's jurisdiction and interference

The United States has a long history of involvement in global affairs, including military interventions, economic sanctions, diplomatic negotiations, and intelligence operations. The US has been involved in conflicts and interactions in many regions of the world, including the middle East, Asia, Latin America, and Africa, to advance its strategic and economic interests.

Promoting democracy, human rights, humanitarian aid, and global stability has been the forefront excuse to its self-interest and geographical considerations. In recent years, the US's role in the world has been more intensified and clearer with advocating for a more restrained foreign policy and greater emphasis on multilateralism and diplomacy. The Trump's Administration, for example, pursued an "America First" foreign policy which sought to prioritize US interest over global engagement and corporation (Ettinger, 2018).

US's foreign policies are driven by a complex set of factors, including national security, economic interests, and diplomacy. In pursuing its foreign policy objectives, US has been historically using a variety of tactics, such as military intervention, economic sanctions, and alliances with other countries.

During the Cold War, the Us and its allies NATO (North Atlantic Treaty Organization) to counter the Soviet Union's influence in Europe, provided economic and military aid to countries in the developing world to prevent them falling under Soviet control.
There have been instances where the US Government's motives to engage in military conflicts, invasions or wars have been questioned or viewed as abuse of power or bullying.

Few examples:

In 1915, US invaded and occupied Haiti and established control over Haiti's government and economy, The US government justified its intervention as necessary to restore order and protect American interests in Haiti, which was experiencing political instability and economic turmoil at time (Department of State Office of the Historian, Milestones: 1914-1920.

Eventually after they left the country in 1935, left Haiti emptied handed, re-structured all Haiti's institutions, economy, and constitutions to operate only for the benefits and or interests of US government or the deep state. While the US Propaganda is to help Haiti in distress, the occupation was highly marked by repression, human rights abuses, and forced labor and extrajudicial killings.

In 1964, Present Lyndon B. Johnson claimed that two US Navy destroyers were attacked by North Vietnamese vessels in the Gulf of Tonkin. Therefore, the US Congress authorized the use of military force in Vietnam. It was later on revealed that the incident was exaggerated and possibly fabricated.

In 2003, The US led a coalition of countries to invade Iraq. Iraq was condemned to be destroyed because President Saddam Hussein possessed weapons of mass destruction and posed a threat to global security. After Iraq was invaded with significant amount of destruction, no weapon of mass destruction was found. The US government or deep state manipulated the situation with lies to drag allies to war and justify the invasion.

In 2011, The US invaded Afghanistan after the 9/11 attacks in US soil stating that the Taliban government was harboring terrorists which was a threat to US. Critics argued that the US government's true motives were all about securing control of Afghanistan's natural resources, including its opium trades, and establishing a foothold in the region.

Since 2014 the US has been deeply involved in the Syrian War by providing support to anti-government (so-called labeled) rebel groups and carrying out airstrikes against targets associated with the Syrian government and its allies (Parenti, 2001). The US advanced that its involvement is motivated by a desire to combat terrorism and support democratic values. However, one can conclude that the US does nothing but fuel and prolong the conflicts and contribute to civilian casualties.

The deep state various viewpoints

In the case of an **individual or citizen** of a country, it can be seen as the force that influences the lawmakers to make laws and regulations that are clear and proven detrimental to the population and still the lawmakers cannot change them, don't do anything about them, or simply look the other way around. Certain citizens may see such circumstances as if those so-called lawmakers are told what they can talk about, say or do. It's as if those lawmakers have set boundaries that they cannot cross. It can even be seen as if their primary duties are more to that invisible force instead of the people whom they presumed to be working for. Based on your memories and understanding, you can certainly recall some examples that fit this situation.

In the case of an **activist** (let the activist be the person or group of persons standing against that visible or invisible force in attempt to preserve autonomy, sovereignty, or values of the institution or country which is the victim of that force of terror) or passivist (let the passivist be the person or group of individuals or institutions who ease that force of terror to go through on the population either by complicity, greed, ignorance, or weakness). The activist may see the Deep State as the biggest and most difficult barrier for the common people to live a dignified life which consists of:

The people have access to necessities of life, such as food, shelter, healthcare, and security. They have autonomy, sovereignty, and freedom to make choices and decisions about their own lives, future, and country. The activists are well informed of the power and evilness of that force of terror, still they pursue their goal at the expenses of defaming, destroying, and even killing them. In the case of a **foreign country or a third world country**, it can be compared to an earthquake, a cyclone, or a natural phenomenon against which the country can't do anything as a self-defense due to its superpower.

In the US democratic system, the concept of law and order represents an important pillar of the rule of law and a fundamental aspect of maintaining a functioning democracy (United States Courts). The US government, as a democratic system, has adopted the concept of 'law and order,' which is an important pillar and a fundamental aspect of maintaining a functioning democratic system. Law and order are referred to the system of rules, regulations, and institutions that are designed to maintain public safety and social stability within the United States. It also includes laws and regulations that govern various aspects of social behavior, such as criminal law, civil, and regulatory law. Therefore, the US government has a range of forces and institutions dedicated to maintaining law and order within the country. They are classified as federal and state law. First are the federal law enforcement agencies which is made of the Federal Bureau of Investigation (FBI), the Drug Enforcement Administration (DEA), and the Bureau of Alcohol, Tobacco, Firearms and Explosives (ATF). Last are the state and local law enforcement agencies such as, police departments, sheriff's offices, and state troopers. Both the state and federal levels, combined, make it a robust system to maintain law and order by ensuring that those who violate the law are held accountable. This important pillar "law and order" of the US government justice system reinforces the principle 'no one is above the law' which is a cornerstone of the American Justice system and enshrined in the Constitution.

The main objective of this essential and fundamental principle is to establish a system of check and balances which is designed to prevent any one person or group from becoming too powerful. As such, its role in a true democratic system and its impartial application are essential to maintaining the rule of law and preserving the integrity of democratic institutions.

From birth, the US Colonies have been a symbol of power as the colony leaders revolted from England's unjust treatment. Till today, the US government has been and remained in power, so much that it is the most powerful country on earth in the past century. Some of the contributing factors that make US government a powerful empire is its large and technologically advanced military, its strong economy, its global cultural influence, and its role as a leader in the international diplomacy and alliances. The US military possesses some of the most sophisticated technology and weapons system in the world. They are advanced aircrafts, ships, submarines, and ground-based equipment. The US is highly skilled at operating in complex and challenging environments, such as desert or jungle terrain, and can operate in multiple theaters simultaneously (Ikenberry, 2001).

Nationally, the US has a robust network of air and missile defense systems, advanced surveillance and reconnaissance capabilities, and highly trained and skilled personnel. With its extensive network of military bases and deployment capabilities, the US military is capable to respond quickly to any potential threats. Thus, the US defense system has whatever tool needed at its disposal to defend the country against any potential domestic or foreign threats.

Internationally, US uses its advanced technology and weapons systems, and its network of military bases and forward-deployed personnel to project power and respond quickly to potential threats across the globe. Moreover, the US robust intelligence community is capable to gather and analyze information from around the world. This intelligence is used to identify potential threats and inform military decision-making, which allows US to more effectively plan and execute military operations.

Tremendous resources readily available, exceptionally well-trained professionals, and widely spread strategic intelligence distinguish US from all others to be the superpower with all necessary means to achieve its objectives whether operating domestically or internationally. US objectives can be summarized as aiming to ensure national security, promoting economic prosperity, uploading democratic values and human rights, exerting global leadership, fostering regional stability, and combating terrorism and weapons proliferation.

Since its inception, the United States has embraced some objectives that has shaped its values, narrative, and way of living. However, the pursuit of these objectives has been often left a bitter aftertaste wherever the US has acted. This is evident in numerous wars initiated or participated in by US over the past century. In a previous chapter, I highlighted several unnecessary wars created by US based on false justifications. Remarkably, it is difficult to remember a war between two or more countries where the US did not play a role either as aggressor, catalyst, or invader. With such behavioral history or abuse of power, one can elude that US is bullying, harassing, and terrorizing other countries to conduct its business oversea. The US assets the right to intervene in any country affair legally when convenient or covertly if entry is prohibited, assuming the role of the world's righteous judge, the global police force, with its soil serving as the supreme courthouse. Consequently, the US has engaged in covert activities in numerous countries, often instigating civil unrest and branding true patriots as rebels or terrorists. Throughout history, the US has utilized its resources, strategies, and miliary forces to pursue its desires and objectives anywhere in the world; and regardless of the resulting consequences, damages, harm caused, or genocide, the US has relentlessly pursued and achieved its goals (Parenti, 2001). In many instances, this has left a sour taste in the form of arbitrary arrests of foreign citizens (excluding legal extradition), the assassination of patriots, including heads of states, and the physical destruction of countries through ground weapons, airstrikes, or bombs. Furthermore, the US has contributed to destabilizing institutions and normalizing corruption and immorality, all under the guise of protecting American interests and promoting democracy through supposed humanitarian aid.

Chapter XI
The Championship Games.

Ladies and gentlemen, boys and girls, close your eyes and transport yourself to the colossal stadium, where a palpable sense of anticipation fills the air, electrifying every nerve in your body. Feel the pulsating energy reverberating through the stands as you anxiously await the grand entrance of two extraordinary teams, poised to engage in an epic battle for the ultimate championship glory.

On one side of the arena stands, a titan, a team with an illustrious history of triumph, both on a national and international stage. They have conquered mountains, shattered records, and amassed a treasure trove of accolades, harnessing every conceivable resource at their disposal. Their name echoes through the annals of world history, their dominance leaving opponents quaking in fear.

However, amidst the sea of unyielding might, emerges a beacon of hope, an underdog/outsider team determined to etch their name in the hallowed halls of greatness. They defy the odds, armed with sheer determination, an unwavering belief in their abilities, and an unshakeable tenacity. This David against Goliath tale weaves a tapestry of passion, resilience, and unbridled courage as they strive to vanquish the indomitable force that has yet to taste defeat.

As the countdown begins, a symphony of emotions cascades through the crowd not to say the world. Hearts pound in unison, synchronized with the palpitations of a nation longing for a hero, yearning for that moment of unadulterated triumph. It is a collision of dreams and aspirations, a clash of legends and underdogs, where tenacity, resilience, and perseverance dare to defy the cold logic of statistics and forecasts.

The battle lines are drawn, and the stage is set for an epic spectacle that will reverberate through time. Every pass, every strike/shot, and every goal becomes a brushstroke on the canvas of destiny, painting a tale of triumph, heartache, and the relentless pursuit of greatness. This is more than just a game; it's a clash of titans, a dance of emotions, and a celebration of the human spirit pushing beyond boundaries. For in this grand arena of society, history will be rewritten, legends will be born, and the world will bear witness to an awe-inspiring saga of triumph against insurmountable odds. Welcome to a spectacle that will stir your soul/imagination, leaving an indelible mark on your being, forever reminding you of the boundless power of the human spirit.

And the moment we've all been waiting for has finally arrived! Please open your eyes, awaken your mind, and wave your emotions! This David against Goliath tale is manifested in the case of Mr. Donald J Trump characterized as David, the shepherd with a sling and a stone versus the United States of America being Goliath, the warrior with javelins, spears, swords, and large shields.

Two formidable teams, renowned for their tenacity and skills, converged upon the revered battleground, poised to etch their names into the annals of world history. This extraordinary clash, the war of the century, represents an unparalleled struggle for honor and greatness, as the perceived underdog seeks to overthrow the seemingly invincible force and ascend to the throne. Meanwhile, the undefeated world champion valiantly defends their prestigious title, ensuring their legacy remains unchallenged. Can this underdog truly defy the odds and emerge triumphant against the indomitable force that has crushed all who dared to oppose it? Will the outsider, a novice in the face of this supremely powerful adversary, be the one to elude defeat? Can this ingenious mastermind ascend to unimaginable heights, establishing themselves as an untouchable champion? While the believers possess unwavering faith, skeptics harbor doubts, yet this underdog, the incumbent, and the outsider possess an unquenchable fire, burning within, to etch his name in the pantheon of world legends.

Mr. Donald Trump has tirelessly traversed the path to the championship, earning his rightful place in the grand finale of world history. Through his reputation as an exemplary warrior. No individual is better equipped than him to confront Team USA, the formidable deep state that has dominated the field for a considerable period. Team USA has remained unbeaten across all the battlefields it has encountered since its inception as a nation. No opposing country has emerged victorious in any military conflict or war against them. It is a testament to the adage that "might makes right."

Both the United States and Donald Trump were destined for greatness. The American colonies boldly revolted against and defied Great Britain, birthing the United States, while Donald, from a young age, exhibited championship qualities by requiring a distinct learning environment that surpassed his peers.

The United States, as a global superpower, has historically played a pivotal role in maintaining law and order both domestically and internationally. The United States has utilized its powerful system to ensure that no one is above the law, focusing on its actions and initiatives within its borders and on the international stage. Domestically US has established a robust legal framework that upholds the principle of equality before the law. The U.S. Constitution, along with federal, state, and local laws, form the foundation of the American legal system.

US actively engages in international efforts in collaboration with transnational organizations, such as the United Nations and Interpol, to promote global security and enforce international law. Although the US is not a party to the International Criminal Court (ICC) (ICC list of States parties to the Rome Statute), it has cooperated with the court on certain cases to protect the American interest.

In the wake of 9/11 terrorist attacks, the United States implemented various measures to combat terrorism both domestically and internationally. These include the establishment of the Department of Homeland Security, enhanced intelligence sharing with partner nations, and targeted military operations against terrorist groups.

The US employs economic sanctions as a tool to maintain international law and order. Sanctions are imposed on the countries or individuals involved in activities such as terrorism, human rights abuses, nuclear proliferation, or cyberattacks, aiming to illegal behavior and compliance with international norms. US Department of states, Office of Economic Sanctions Policy and Implementation as at the time of preparing this book, lists sanctions on Belarus, Burma, Burundi, Central African Republic, Cuba, Democratic People's Republic of Korea, Democratic Republic of the Congo, Iran and several others. Some of these are recent while some have existed since as far back as the 70s (US Department of State).

The United States, known as the most powerful nation in the world from its inception, has embraced the eagle as its emblem, symbolizing its dominance among all birds with its two wings. Domestically, one wing represents the federal, state, and local authorities, including the police, undercover FBI agents, and specialized law enforcement teams, whose role is to maintain order and security. The other wing extends internationally, encompassing allied countries, ambassadors, military bases, and the spreading of the American dream. This establishment of power has positioned the United States as the most formidable and flamboyant figure of superiority in modern civilization.

Whether within its borders or beyond, the United States has utilized various means, such as diplomacy, intelligence, sanctions, military forces, and the justice system, to control or eliminate individuals who pose a threat to democratic principles or disrupt law and order. The US team has a long-standing track record of emerging victorious in all the wars it has engaged in (Mansoor, 2019), conquering and subduing the word with direct or indirect blows. Notable achievements include defeating the Soviet Union, Vietnam, Japan, Iraq, Afghanistan, President Daniel Noriega of Panama, Osama Bin Laden, General Gadhafi of Libya, mob boss John Gandhi, Timothy Matvey, and countless others. Th US team has consistently displayed unparalleled strength and resilience.

Both domestically and internationally, the United States has never been better equipped than it is today. Its intelligence agencies possess state-of-art technological resources essential for controlling or eliminating threats, be they individuals, gangsters, or entire nations. In essence, one could say that the formula for success can be expressed as "intelligence plus capability equals victory." This is why the United States has stood as the greatest and strongest champion to date.

Despite its notable strength and resilience, and its history of emerging victorious in past conflicts, the US team has yet to effectively challenge the businessman and celebrity persona, the 45th President of the United States, and the potential 47th President of the United States of America, Donald J Trump. Trump has managed to navigate his way around the governing principles of the US team and the notion that no one is above the law. Whether in business, entertainment, or politics, he has repeatedly defied or circumvented laws without facing the same consequences as others who have crossed the US team. Trump's ability to manipulate the law without being held accountable sets him apart from the usual course of justice. Despite the bitter taste he has left in the mouths of many individuals, institutions, and the US government though his dealing in various fields, he has largely evaded penalties even when it is evident that he has broken or abused the law. Trump's intelligence, influence, and skill have allowed him to challenge the status quo of the established American democratic system, exerting his power at all levels, even to the point of inciting a coup.

While the US team's democratic guiding principle of "No one is above the law" holds true for most, it does not apply to Donald Trump, as he has managed to outsmart the American system. Although those in his inner circle who have aided his rise to power have encountered legal troubles, Trump himself has lived above the law. Regardless of the criticisms surrounding Trump's character and reputation, an impartial and thorough analysis of his strategy reveals that he is a cunning champion who has played the games by his own rules and terms, while the US justice system watches him rise unchecked.

Donald Trump has become an unrivaled champion who remains untouched and undefeated by the powerful and feared US team. Being an innovative genius and an innate champion, he understood the importance of assembling a loyal, competent, and courageous team to execute his agenda. Over time, he has built his dream team and achieved victory after victory. While he continues to be an untouchable and undefeated champion, many members of his team have paid a heavy price. Whether it was a misdemeanor or a felony, imprisonment or loss of career and licenses, remorse or repentance, the entire team has borne the burden (LaFraneire, 2019; Epstein, 2022) while he remains unscathed, cementing his status as the champion of the century. Indeed, most of Trump's team have faced significant legal troubles, some were caught in illicit actions, while others fell prey to the established US Justice system. According to the democratic principle of checks and balances, where no one is above the law, all these players have faced consequences.

Some of charges and consequences levied against them were:

1. Trump's personal lawyer, the one-time fixer for Trump, Michael Cohen, charged with a series of crimes, most notably secret hush-money payments made during the final months of the 2016 presidential campaign to two women alleging affairs with Trump. As a result of that he was disbarred and lost his law license (Nevett, 2022).
2. Trump's campaign manager, Paul Manafort was charged on count of conspiracy against the US and on one count of conspiracy to obstruct justice due to attempts to tamper with witnesses. He was sentenced to 47 months in prison (Lafraniere, 2019). There are images from the press of Manafort in court wearing handcuffs in New York City. His time as Trump campaign manager exposed him to scrutiny over his consulting works. Further investigations culminated in a case with Justice Department that cost him 3.15 million dollars settlement fee (Concepcion, 2023).
3. Trump's national security adviser, Army lieutenant general Michael Flynn pleaded guilty to lying to the FBI about his

contacts with Russia during the presidential transition. His sentenced is still pending after serving time in jail (Zurcher, 2020). He's tenure as the national security adviser only lasted 23 days, after which he was forced out. He faced further scrutiny over declaration of payments received for giving speeches and consulting for lobbyists from Russian and Turkey.

4. Brian Kolfage pleaded guilty to misappropriation of funds raised for the "We Build the Wall" campaign. He was sentenced to 4-¼ years in prison in April 2023 alongside Andrew Badolato (Cohen, 2023). Contrary to the promise not to take any salary or compensation from the money raised for the wall, evidence presented showed that this was an orchestrated plan to defraud donors who numbered in thousands. The evidence showed how they made deliberate attempt to lie and hide the funds diverted (United States Attorney's Office, Southern District of New York, 2023). The abuse of the trust of donors, this is a big stain on their reputation. It was also stated that this crime will affect willingness of donors to political campaign. So not only did this affect the reputation of the offenders, but it also had a wider impact on the party and American politics.

5. Trump's inaugural committee chair Tom Barrack was charged on seven counts on the idea that Barrack used his closeness to Trump to advance the direction of senior UAE officials. He was later acquitted in November 2022 (Cohen, 2022). Despite being acquitted, during the investigation text messages between Tom Barrack and a businessman who was well connected with UAE rulers were exposed. Other information about dealings also came to light and this is obvious detriment to his reputation and influence.

6. Trump's 2016 presidential campaign top fundraiser, Elliott Broldy was charged with conspiracy for failing to register and disclose his role in a lobbying effort aimed at stopping a criminal investigation into massive fraud at a Malaysian investment fund and advocating for the removal of a Chinese billionaire living in the US. A sentence is yet to be imposed (Hosenbakk, 2020). He was later pardoned by Donald Trump as part of his presidential pardon (Duggan, 2023). He was made to openly

testify and admit his failed attempt. So not only was he disgraced for his illegal acts, his incompetence at executing his intentions were exposed. He cooperated with authorities to expose others involved in criminal cases relating to Malaysian sovereign wealth fund.

7. Trump's 2016 deputy to the campaign chairman, Rick Gates was charged with aiding and abetting Paul Manafort in concealing $75 million in foreign bank accounts. Rick Gates was sentenced to 45 days in jail. He later cooperated with the authorities to help convict Paul Manafort and Roger Stone in the case relating to Russian interference in US politics. While this might be regarded as being of service to the government. It is expected that being instrumental in the conviction of his associates may bave had some negative impact on trust and relationship within the inner circle. Perhaps this is intentional tactic to create and maintain division within Trump's inner circle.

8. Trump's 2016 presidential campaign informal foreign policy adviser, George Nader was charged with two counts of sex crimes involving minors. He was sentenced to 10 years in prison for being found in possession of child pornography and for transporting a 14-year-old boy, a minor, from Czech Republic to his home in the US for sex (Buchman, 2020). An article by the Independent in 2020 described him as a "lifelong pedophile". He was the president and editor of the Middle East Insight, a media outlet. Which has now been negatively affected by the ruined reputation. He appeared in court in prison gear and details of his gross acts with child pornography were revealed. It also came to light that he had previously been convicted to 6 months in prison for similar offenses relating to child pornography. His connections with a powerful player in the UAE were key to his role in Trump's inner circle. For example, he helped secure a meeting between Trump's associates and the crown prince (Buchman, 2020).

9. Trump's 2016 campaign junior adviser, George Papadopoulos was lying to investigators about his contacts with individuals tied to Russia. He was sentenced to 12 days in prison for lying

to the FBI in the Mueller probe into Russia's interference with the US elections. He was arrested in 2017 for lying to the FBI that he had contacts which turned out to be false. He claimed to have had contact with people like Putin's cousin, Russian ambassadors, and the nature of his connection with Joseph Mifsud. He was also charged with obstruction of justice by deleting his social media account (Frank 2019).

10. Trump's ally in 2016 campaign, Roger Stone was convicted of lying to Congress and threatening a witness regarding his efforts for Trump's campaign. He was sentenced to three years and four months in prison. The self-confessed political dirty trickster had been a Trump adviser for a long time. He had been in politics since 1972 during the time of Nixon. Alongside Paul Manafort and Charles Black, he ran a lobbying firm in Washington in the 80s with clients including the former president of Zaire, Mobutu Sese Seko, George W Bush, and Donald Trump (Pengelly, 2022). Roger Stone faced indictment during the Robert Mueller investigation. In protest against the harshness of the sentence of seven to nine years imprisonment that Stone was initially given, four prosecutors resigned. He was eventually granted clemency by Trump. Stone does not seem to be apologetic about his reputation as a political "dirty trickster". At some point, he had a documentary team following him about in a "Stop the Steal" program. An open attempt at overturning the election result in Trump's favour (Lowell, 2022).

11. Trump Organization's long-time chief financial officer, Allen Weissenberg was charged with tax crimes tied to perks he was given in lieu of salary. He was sentenced to 5 months in prison. He was also made to testify against Trump organization for tax fraud. He had worked at the Trump Organization for much of his career since the 80s. It came to light that he enjoyed perks such as luxury apartments and luxury cars thanks to tax evasion. It was estimated that his unpaid taxes and refunds on a false basis came to around $900,000 (Miller, 2023). According to his confession Trump and his family members were not aware of his tax crimes. Therefore, this is likely to have put a

dent in his relationship with the Trump Organization and his retirement plan.

Donald Trump consistently aims for the highest, most extravagant, and most valuable rewards in life. Rather than being consumed by fear or worries, he derives enjoyment from navigating through hardships. If a challenge or battle doesn't appear impossible, it simply isn't worth his time or energy. With his extensive arsenal, expertise (magna cum laude) in the American democratic system, and a mindset geared towards winning (TRP shot), I firmly believe that Donald Trump will discover or forge a path within the American democratic system to absolve himself of all pending charges. This achievement would undoubtedly set yet another unprecedented record in world history.

Donald Trump thrives on challenging norms, pushing boundaries, and setting new records. It's clear that it's in his nature to take on seemingly insurmountable challenges that others have never dared to attempt, thereby establishing himself as the sole capable individual in various endeavors. He has already achieved records that no one else has dared to touch.

A newly proposed characteristic of charismatic leaders is now being used to shed light on Donald Trump's leadership style. In 2023, Jumel Pluviose summarized this trait as follows: "Charismatic leaders envision the final goal or endpoint, while others rally to embrace, adapt, refine, and work together to bring that vision to fruition." In the context of Donald Trump's leadership, it's evident that he possesses the ability to harness his genius and astute understanding of the system to assemble a capable team of individuals who can guide him toward victory. This team comprises experts, professionals, and ardent supporters, all united in their collective effort to bring his vision to life. While Donald Trump may not have all the answers at every step of the journey, his unwavering confidence in his ultimate success is a hallmark of his charismatic leadership style.

In conclusion, Donald Trump has emerged as an indomitable and formidable champion who fearlessly challenges the established governmental establishment on all fronts. He has shattered the boundaries of the status quo, disrupting the very essence of the motto: law and order. Despite facing numerous controversies and legal hurdles, Donald Trump has demonstrated an uncanny ability to transcend the notion of being above the law. While his team members have encountered significant legal troubles, including charges, convictions, imprisonment, and the loss of careers or licenses, Trump himself has emerged unscathed, firmly establishing his position as the unparalleled champion of the century.

In any endeavor, whether it's a sporting event, championship, war, game, fight, or even a legal case, victory or defeat remains uncertain until the final outcome is determined. In essence, nothing is certain until the last moment of the competition or until the legal judgment is rendered.

This unparalleled prowess to skillfully navigate the American system and elude the consequences that typically befall others in similar circumstances is a testament to Trump's unwavering intelligence, profound influence, and remarkable expertise in challenging the established democratic norms. His ability to confront the mighty force of the United States and emerge triumphant showcases his exceptional capabilities as a champion who has left an indelible mark on the annals of history.

Section III
Donald J Trump with an indelible legacy
Chapter XII
Donald Trump's Legacy

What is a Legacy?

Legacy refers to the lasting impact or imprint left behind by an individual or an entity, encompassing their notable achievements, actions, and influence that shape the course of history. Donald Trump, the businessman, the celebrity persona, and the 45th President of the United States, whether early or later, positive and or negative aspects that have defined his tenure, has an indelible legacy. From 2017 to 2021, Donald Trump's presidency left an indelible mark on American democracy, prompting an in-depth analysis of his various actions and their consequences.

An Evaluation of Trump's impact and legacy.

Trump's presidency was marked by controversy, polarizing policies, and a unique style of leadership. A thorough review of his domestic and foreign policies and COVID-19 response is presented below.

Domestic policy

Economy:

A. Tax Reform was one of Trump's major accomplishments. This legislation lowered the corporate tax rate from 35% to 21%, reduced individual income tax rates, and eliminated certain deductions. The passage of tax cuts and jobs Act 2017 was a major milestone for his administration (Trumpwhitehousearchives).

B. Trade Policy was characterized by a focus on protecting American workers and reducing the trade deficit. He renegotiated several trade deals, including the North Americn Free Trade Agreement (NAFTA) (Chatszky, McBride and Sergie, 2020), and implemented tariffs on Chinese imports.

C. Economic Growth: Trump's economic policies contributed to a period of economic growth, with unemployment reaching historic lows and the stock market reaching record highs prior to to the COVID-19 pandemic (Randewich and AHmed, 2020).

Healthcare

A. Affordable Care Act: Trump attempted to repeal and replace the Affordable Care Act (ACA) but was unsuccessful. However, his administration did eliminate the indicidual mandate, which required individuals to have health insurance or face a penalty (Stolberg, 2020).

B. Opioid Crisis: Trump declared the opioid epidemic a public health emergency and implemented various measures to address it, such as increasing access to treatment and expanding the availability of overdose-reversal drugs (Wen and Sadeghi, 2020).

Immigration

A. Trump's policies on immigration were characterized by a focus on border security. He implemented a travel ban on several predominantly Muslim countries, increased deportations, and built a wall along the southern border (Trump Whitehouse Archives-Immigration).

B. DACA: Trump attempted to end the Deferred Action for Childhood Arrivals (DACA) program, which provides protection for undocumented immigrants who were brought to the US as children. However, his attempts were blocked by the courts.

Foreign Policy

Middle East

A. Israel: Trump moved the us embassy in Israel to Jerusalem, recognized Israeli sovereignty over the Golan Heights, and brokered peace deals between Israel and several Arab states.
B. Iran: Trump ordered airstrikes against the Syrian government in response to chemical weapons attacks and withdrew US troops from Syria.

Asia

A. North Korea: Trump held two summits with North Korean Leader Kim Jong-un to negotiate the denuclearization of the Korean peninsula.
B. China: Trump implemented tariffs on Chinese imports and engaged in a trade war with China (Hass and Denmark, 2020).

Europe

A. NATO: Trump criticized NATO allies for not contribution enough to the alliance and threatened to withdraw from the organization.
B. Russia: Trump's relationship with Russia was controversial, with allegations of collusion with Russia during the 2016 election.

COVID-19 Response

Trump's response to the COVID-19 pandemic was criticized for being slow and inadequate. He downplayed the severity of the virus, promoted unproven treatments, and criticized state governors who implemented lockdowns and mask mandates. His administration also faced criticism for its handling of vaccine distribution.

Trump's impact on American society and politics also extended beyond his policies and initiatives. His rhetoric and behavior often fueled divisions and tensions, particularly in the wake of the 2020 presidential election, which he repeatedly claimed was fraudulent.

In terms of his legacy, Trump's tenure as president is likely to be remembered as one of the most polarizing and divisive in American history. While his supporters praise him for his efforts to stimulate economic growth and restore American leadership on the global stage, his critics argue that his presidency undermined democracy, inflamed social tensions, and weakened America's position in the world. Ultimately, the full impact and legacy of Donald Trump's presidency are likely to be debated and analyzed for years to come.

Economically, Trump's legacy is often associated with his emphasis on deregulation and tax cuts, which proponents argue stimulated business growth, job creation, and a booming stock market. Additionally, his administration pursued trade policies focused on protecting American industries and renegotiating international agreements, such as NAFTA, resulting in the USMCA trade deal.

On the other hand, Trump's legacy is also marked by controversial and polarizing decisions. His rhetoric and communication style were often criticized for exacerbating divisions within society. His immigration policies, including the travel ban and family separation at the border, drew widespread condemnation and sparked heated debates on human rights and immigration reform. Additionally, Trump's handling of the COVID-19 pandemic remains a significant aspect of his legacy, with opinions varying on the effectiveness of his administration's response.

Beyond policy, Donald Trump's legacy extends to his role in shaping the political landscape, particularly within the Republican Party. His unconventional campaign and subsequent presidency highlighted the power of populism and the influence of social media in modern politics. Trump's strong appeal to his base and ability to command media attention brought attention to issues often overlooked by mainstream politics. It is my belief that his experiment on the American political establishment will take no time for his legacy to take effect immediately in the upcoming elections and administrations. Some of the ways are:

Ridiculing and Humiliating Opponents

Throughout his presidency, Donald Trump was notorious for his penchant for ridiculing and humiliating his political opponents. Through the use of derogatory nicknames and engaging in personal attacks, Trump fostered a hostile and divisive political climate. While some of his supporters may have appreciated his unfiltered style, it only served to exacerbate the nation's polarization and impede constructive political discourse. His success with this approach has set a precedent, potentially paving the way for others who might employ similar tactics in pursuit of their own success. This "Trumpism" style could potentially alter the civility of debates, campaigns, or administrations, thus becoming a part of his legacy.

Unfiltered Communication Style

Another defining characteristic of Trump's presidency was his unfiltered communication style. He frequently spoke without adhering to the relevance of the topic at hand, which attracted substantial media attention. This approach enabled him to dominate news cycles, communicate directly with his base, and achieve his objectives. However, it also garnered criticism for its lack of nuance, coherence, and adherence to factual accuracy, ultimately eroding the credibility of the presidential office. Some may argue that in today's post-truth era, where credibility may not hold as much significance, this style of communication could be considered a defining aspect of the post-Donald Trump era, regardless of its impact on objectivity.

Questioning the Integrity of the Election System

One of the most contentious aspects of Trump's legacy was his consistent questioning and challenging of the integrity and honesty of the election system. Despite a lack of substantial evidence, he propagated unfounded claims of widespread voter fraud, which sowed doubt among his supporters (given their trust in his leadership for firsthand information) and eroded confidence in democratic processes. This ultimately reached its zenith with the January 6, 2021, insurrection at the United States Capitol.

Trump's devoted supporters exhibited an unwavering loyalty to him due to his charismatic appeal. The question arises: could the mentality of "Why not follow Trump's path, since I'm losing anyway" become a new approach for future candidates? If it does, how might this alter the landscape of democracy and the behavior of other candidates?
Disregard for Institutional Norms

Trump's presidency was characterized by a notable disregard for institutional norms in pursuit of his personal agenda. He frequently sidestepped conventional channels and norms, relying on executive orders, social media, and unilateral actions to advance his policy objectives. While some supporters praised his capacity to challenge the established order, critics contended that this approach eroded democratic checks and balances and posed a potential threat to the long-term health of democratic institutions.

A concerning thought emerges: if Donald Trump employed these tactics, then others may feel justified in doing the same. If this mentality becomes the prevailing approach to governance, it raises the question of whether the American political system can still be accurately described as democratic.

Influence on Extremist Ideologies

Trump's presidency saw a resurgence of white supremacy and extremist ideologies. His divisive statements and hesitancy to unequivocally condemn extremist groups (Rios, 2022) gave them a sense of legitimacy and bolstered their actions. This troubling development exacerbated societal rifts and posed a significant threat to social cohesion.

If this resurgence were to gain political power, it's easy to imagine the kind of conflict it could engender within the population. Would the same rhetoric that Trump used during his campaign, suggesting that there were "fine people on both sides" when clashes occurred in March, still hold true, or would there be a reevaluation of the consequences of such rhetoric on national unity and stability?

Associations with Totalitarian World Leaders

Donald Trump's bold association with totalitarian world leaders, such as North Korea's Kim Jong-un and Russia's Vladimir Putin, raised concerns about his approach to global diplomacy. While Trump pursued unconventional diplomatic strategies, critics argued that his warm relations with autocratic leaders undermined American values and human rights advocacy on the global stage (Chodakiewicz, 2018). The American democracy does associate or ally with autocratic leaders when it's convenient. Donald Trump does it his way and differently which upsets the conventional democracy.

Impact on the Concept of the Deep State

Trump's presidency was characterized by his narrative of combating the "deep state" – a perceived network of entrenched bureaucrats and officials seeking to undermine his administration. While this narrative resonated with some supporters, it also contributed to an erosion of trust in government institutions and their ability to function impartially. Trump's claims of a deep state have opened the door for subsequent politicians to exploit similar rhetoric, potentially undermining democratic governance. I wondered if the adage "Nothing last forever" would find its meaning that that invincible and invisible force behind the American democracy is about to be revealed and weakened. Only time knows.

Immigration and Border Security

Trump's stance on immigration and border security was a central pillar of his presidency. His administration implemented controversial policies such as family separations at the border and attempted to restrict travel from several predominantly Muslim countries. This approach drew widespread criticism from human rights advocates, who argued that it undermined the country's commitment to compassion and inclusivity.

Supreme Court Appointments

One significant aspect of Trump's legacy is his profound impact on the composition of the U.S. Supreme Court. During his presidency, he successfully appointed three justices, fundamentally altering the court's ideological balance towards a more conservative majority. These appointments are expected to have long-lasting effects on legal interpretation and decision-making, especially in pivotal areas such as reproductive rights, gun control, and civil liberties. Notably, Trump leveraged his influence within the Republican-dominated chambers to postpone the filling of a Supreme Court vacancy for over a year following the passing of Justice Antonin Scalia on February 13, 2016. This early maneuver suggests that Trump was already wielding considerable political power even before his inauguration. If this holds true, it underscores the vital importance of the power of influence as a skillset for candidates and leaders to cultivate in contemporary politics.

Response to Global Challenges

Trump's presidency coincided with various global challenges, including climate change, nuclear proliferation, and international conflicts. His decision to withdraw the United States from the Paris Agreement and the Iran nuclear deal, among other international agreements, drew criticism for weakening global cooperation on critical issues. Trump's "America First" approach reshaped the country's role on the global stage, leading to mixed reactions from different stakeholders.

Healthcare Reform

Trump's attempts to repeal and replace the Affordable Care Act (ACA), also known as Obamacare, were a significant policy focus during his presidency (Thomson, 2020). While his administration made efforts to dismantle the ACA, including reducing the individual mandate penalty and promoting alternative healthcare options, a comprehensive healthcare reform plan did not materialize. This issue remains a point of contention and unresolved challenge in American politics.

Response to COVID-19 Pandemic

The COVID-19 pandemic emerged during Trump's presidency and presented a major test of leadership. His administration faced criticism for its initial handling of the crisis, including delays in implementing widespread testing and inconsistent messaging. However, Operation Warp Speed, a government initiative to accelerate vaccine development, achieved remarkable success in facilitating the production and distribution of COVID-19 vaccines.

Legislative Achievements

Assessing Trump's legislative achievements is essential to understanding his impact on policy. Notable accomplishments during his tenure include tax reform, criminal justice reform (First Step Act), and deregulation efforts. While these achievements received varying levels of bipartisan support, Trump's ability to pass significant legislation was limited by political divisions and a lack of consensus in Congress.

In conclusion, Donald Trump's legacy reverberates far beyond the realms previously discussed, as his presidency left an indelible mark on numerous aspects of American governance. By examining his profound influence on economic policies, immigration, the Supreme Court, global challenges, healthcare reform, COVID-19 response, and legislative achievements, we gain a comprehensive understanding of his tenure as the 45th President of the United States. However, his impact extends even further, as his unyielding approach to opponents, unfiltered communication style, challenges to the election system, disregard for institutional norms, associations with extremist ideologies, alliances with totalitarian world leaders, and his profound impact on the concept of the deep state have etched themselves into the annals of history.

Donald Trump's unconventional path has not only left lasting impressions but has also emboldened politicians to follow a similar unorthodox trajectory. While his supporters admired his disruptive nature and perceived strength, critics argue that his actions weakened democratic institutions and exacerbated societal divisions. However, regardless of one's viewpoint, comprehending Trump's legacy is of utmost importance in navigating the challenges and opportunities that lie ahead for American democracy.

By understanding the enduring effects of his actions, we can shape future political discourse and chart the course for policy directions in the United States. It is through this introspection that we can foster a more resilient democracy, addressing the fractures that have emerged and working towards healing the societal wounds that his presidency has brought to the fore.

Donald Trump's legacy is a powerful testament to the forces at play in contemporary politics. It serves as a reminder that leaders have the capacity to transform nations, for better or worse, and that the consequences of their actions reverberate long after they leave office. As we move forward, it is imperative to learn from the past, drawing on the lessons of Trump's presidency to forge a path towards a more inclusive, stable, and prosperous future for all Americans.

Chapter XIII
Conclusion

"The Innovative Genius: The Unparalleled Champion with an Indelible Legacy" offers a comprehensive portrait of Donald Trump's life and career, exploring the multifaceted persona of a man who left an indelible mark on American politics and society. Regardless of readers' political inclinations, this book forces them to confront the complexity of Trump's legacy and its lasting impact on the nation and the world.

One cannot deny that Donald Trump's innovative approach to business, marketing, and political communication transformed the traditional norms of American politics. His ability to connect with a significant portion of the American electorate reflects the changing dynamics of political engagement on the digital age.

While some hail Trump's economic policies for fostering growth and job creation, others criticize his administration for exacerbating divisions within the nation and undermining long-standing diplomatic relationships. Trump's "America First" stance drew both applause and condemnation, depending on one's perspective on nationalism and global engagement.

In evaluating Donald J Trump's legacy, it is crucial to recognize that history will continue to unfold, shaping public perception of his presidency. This book invites readers to engage in a nuanced conversation about the accomplishments, controversies, and complexities surrounding Trump's tenure in the White House.

Ultimately, "The Innovative Genius: The Unparalleled Champion with an Indelible Legacy" encourages readers to critically assess the impact of leadership on society and to ponder the lasting consequences of a leader who challenged conventional norms, whether lauded as a champion of change or critiqued for his methods. Donald Trump's legacy will undoubtedly spark debates for generations to come.

References

ABC News (2006) Donalt Trump: the genius of self-promotion. ABC News

Alfaro M (2022) Bolton says Trump might have pulled the US out of NATO if he had been reelected. The Washington Post

Alexander D (2022) Trump rejoins the forbes 400 a year after falling off the list

American Bankruptcy Institute. Examining Donald Trump's chapter 11 bankruptcies

Baker P, Benner K and Shear MD (2018) Jeff sessions is forced out as attorney general as Trump installs loyalist. The New York Times.

Bausum A (2021) Our Country's presidents: A complete encyclopedia of the U.S. presidency. National Geographic. ISBN-13: 978-1426371998

Beckwith RT (2016) Read Donalt Trump's "America First" foreign policy speech. Time Magazine

Buchman B (2020) Child-sex trafficker from Trump Tower meeting gets 10-year sentence. Courthouse News Service

Chatzky A, McBride J and Sergie MA (2020) NAFTA and the USMCA: weighing the impact of North American trade. Council on Foreign Relations

Chodakiewicz MJ (2018) Trump on a roll: a discussion of his meetings with Kim Jong Un and Vladimir Putin. The Institute of World Politics

Civil Rights Litigation Clearinghouse. Case: United States v. Fred C. Trump, Donald Trump and Trump Management, Inc. 1:73-01529. U.S. District Court for the Eastern District of New York. October 15, 1973 - 1977

Cohen L (2022) Trump ally Barrack acquitted of acting as UAE foreign agent. Reuters

Cohen L (2023) Bannon associate sentenced to 4-¼ years for Trump border wall fraud. Reuters

Concepcion S (2019) Former Trump campaign chairman Paul Manafort settles case with justice department for $3.15M. NBC News

Drenon B (2023) Donald Trump awarded legal fees in Stormy Daniels defamation lawsuit. BBC News

Duggen P (2023) GOP fundraiser says he got millions to illegally lobby Trump administraion. The Washington Post

Epstein K (2022) Steve Bannon sentencing: jail term shows January 6 risks for Trump. BBC News. 21 October 2022   https://www.bbc.com/news/world-us-canada-63350291 accessed 25 January 2023

Ettinger A (2018) Trup's national security strategy. International Journal. 73(3): 474-483

Helmore E (2020) Ex-white house chief of staff John Kelly speaks out against Trump. The Guardian.

Frank TA (2019) The surreal life of George Papadopoulos. The Washington Post. May 20 2019.

Hartmann M (2012) Team Trump brags about picture book's mediocre sales. New York Magazine

Hass R Denmark A (2020) More pain than gain: how the US-China trade war hurt America.Brookings Institut

Hawking S (2009) Illustrated theory of everything: the origin and fate of the universe. Phoenix Books ISBN-13- 978-1597776110 pp 1-117

Igielnik R, Keeter S and Hartig H (2021) Behind Biden's 2020 victory. Pew Research Center.

International Criminal Court. The states parties to the Rome Statue. A-Z listing

Jackson J (2016) Donald Trump named as time magazine's person of the year. The Guardian

Kapur S (2023) Mitt Romney warns Trump is: by far the most likely" GOP nominee in 2024. NBC News.

Karni A and Rogers K (2021) Like father, like son: president Trump lets others mourn. The New York Times

Library of Congress: Presentation U.S. History Primary Source Timeline. Colonial Settlement, 1600s - 1763

LaFraniere S (2019) Rick Gates, Ex-Trump aide and key witness for Mueller, is sentenced to 45 days in jail. The New York Times. 17 December 2019 https://www.nytimes.com/2019/12/17/us/politics/rick-gates-sentencing.html Accessed 26 January 2023

Lipson JC (2016) Making America worse: jobs and money at Trump casinos, 1997-2010. Temple University Legal Studies Research Paper. 2016-47 pp 1-21

Lowell H (2022) Film offers inside look at Roger Stone's 'stop the steal' efforts before January 6. The Guardian

Machamer P and Miller MD (2021) Galileo Galilei. Stanford Encyclopedia of Philosophy.

Mansoor PR (2016) Why can't America win its wars? Hoover Institution

Marchese D (2023) Paul Ryan says even MAGA diehards believe Trump can't win in 2024. The New York Times.

McAdams DP (2020) The strange case of Donald J Trump: A phsychological reckoning. Oxford Academic.

Miller J (2023) Former Donald Trump executive Allen Weiselberg sentenced to 5 months in jail. Financial Times.

Miller ME 50 years later disagreement of young Trump's military academy record. Washington Post

Mohammed A and Heavey S (2018) Trump calls Tillerson "dumb as a rock" and "lazy". Reuters.

Nevett J (2020) Trump's legal battles: how six cases may play out. BBC News. 15 November 2020. Trump's legal battles: How six cases may play out - BBC News

Office of the New York State Attorney General. Letitia James. A.G. Schneiderman statement on final Trump University settlement. April 9, 2018. Attorney Gneral Press Office/ 212-416-8060

Office of the United States Trade Representative. United States- Mexico-Canada Agreement

Office of the Historian: Milestone: 1914-1920. U.S> invasion and occupation of Haiti, 1915-1934

Parentti C (2001) America's Jihad: A history of origins. Social Justice. 28(3):31-38

Pengelly M (2022) Who is Roger Stone, the Trump ally in the January 6 panel's crosshairs? The Guardian

Randewich N and Ahmed SQ (2020) Trump's stock market: a wild four years. Reuters

Reuters Fact Check (2021) Fact check- Trump has been accused of racism by contemporaries prior to presidential campaign. Reuters

Rios E (2022) Trump condemned for dining with white supremacist Nick Fuentes. The Guardian

Rushe D (2020) Trump signs China trade pact and boasts of "the biggest deal ever seen". The Guardian

R.J.E (2017) What is the "deep state"? The Economist

Schwartzmann P an Miller E (2016) Confidential, Incorrigible. Bully: little Donny was a lot like candidate Donald Trump. Washington Post.

Securities and Exchange Commission (2005) Annual report pursuant to section 13 or 15(d) of the securities exchange act of 1934. Trump entertainment resorts inc. Trump entertainment resorts holdings, L.P. Trump entertainment resorts funding, inc. Washington, DC. 20549. Form10-K. https://www.sec.gov/Archives/edgar/data/943320/000119312506053345/d10k.htm accessed 24 January 2023

Shafer BE and Wagner RL (2018) The Trump presidency and the structure of modern American politics. Cambridge University Press- Perspectives on Politics. 17(2): 340-357

Shane II L (2019) Trump made up injury to dodge Vietnam service, his former lawyer testifies. Military Times

Smith G (2008) Isaac Newton. The Stanford Encyclopedia of Philosophy.

Stolberg SG (2020) Trump administration asks supreme court to strike down affordable care act. The New York Times

Telnaes A (2015) Donald Trump, the master of self-promotion. The Washington Post

Thompson FJ (2020) Six ways Trump has sabotaged the affordable care act. Brookings Institution

Trump Whitehouse Archives (2019) President Donald J Trump's historic tax cuts are delivering real savings and creating more opportunity for all Americans.

Trump Whitehouse Arcchives - Immigration. Administrative Achievements: Achieving a secure border

United States Attorney's Office. Southern District of New York (2023) Two sentenced to prison for 'We Build The wall' online fundraising fraud scheme. Press Release April 26 2023

United State Courts Educational Resources: Overview- Rule of Law

US Department of State. Economic Santions Programs - Listing

United States Department of State. Office of the Hisotrian. Milestones: 1776-1783. The Declaration of Independence, 1776

Vonyo T (2008) Post-war reconstruction and the golden age of economic growth. European Review of Economic History. 12(2):221-241

Wen LS and Sadeghi NB (2020) The opioid crisis and the 2020 US election: crossroads for a national epidemic. Lancet. 396(10259):1316-1318

World Bank Archives: July 1944: Bretton Woods Conference
Zurcher A (2020) Ex-Trump adviser Micheal Flynn charges of lying to FBI dropped. BBC News
116th Congress (2019-2020) H.Res 755- impeaching Donald John Trump, president of the United States, for high crimes and misdemeanors.
117th Congress (2021-2022) H.Res. 24- impeaching Donald John Trump, president of the United States, for high crimes and misdemeanors.